Flash 5 Visual JumpStart

Flash 5™ Visual JumpStart™

Patricia Hartman

San Francisco ◆ Paris ◆ Düsseldorf ◆ Soest ◆ London

Associate Publisher: Cheryl Applewood
Contracts and Licensing Manager: Kristine O'Callaghan
Acquisitions and Developmental Editor: Mariann Barsolo
Editor: Judy Flynn
Production Editor: Nathan Whiteside
Technical Editor: Daniel Gray
Book Designer: Maureen Forys, Happenstance Type-O-Rama
Electronic Publishing Specialist: Maureen Forys, Happenstance Type-O-Rama
Proofreaders: Laurie O'Connell, Nancy Riddiough
Indexer: Ted Laux
CD Technician: Keith McNeil
CD Coordinator: Kara Eve Schwartz
Cover Designer: Daniel Ziegler
Cover Illustrator/Photographer: Daniel Ziegler

Library of Congress Card Number: 00-109119

ISBN: 0-7821-2892-0

Manufactured in the United States of America

10 9 8 7 6 5 4 3 2 1

To my husband, William Rupp, and my family (Mark, Craig, Karina, Deborah, Kent, Serena, Laurissa, Ryan, Sam, Giovanna, Deanna, Laithe, Andrew, and Aunt Florence), whose patience and understanding helped me along the way.

Special thanks must go to that illustrious pair Max and Sasha, who provided so much material for this book. Their tireless efforts in the Mars Mission movie featured in Chapters 8 and 9 are much appreciated.

Acknowledgments

The person primarily responsible for the launching of this project deserves special thanks. This person is my agent, David Fugate, of Waterside Productions. He has been an excellent advocate and advisor.

Mariann Barsolo was also extremely reassuring and encouraging in the beginning and also helpful and understanding throughout the project. Both she and the editors, Nathan Whiteside and Judy Flynn, have been most helpful. A special thanks goes to Judy Flynn, since her eagle eye is responsible for the very concise and precise manuscript. Everyone at Sybex has been very understanding and accepting of the issues that crop up in an endeavor as complex as this one.

Also, I appreciate very much having help from the technical editor, Daniel Gray, who provided the testing that every technical author needs.

Thanks, also, to all of those behind-the-scenes people at Sybex who worked to produce *Flash 5 Visual JumpStart* and to make it succeed.

Contents

Introduction

This book is intended for the beginner. No previous knowledge or use of imaging or animation applications is assumed. Terminology is explained and instructions are explicit. This is a tutorial. After the introductory chapters, each chapter includes a step-by-step presentation of the creation of a sample movie. The reader should follow the steps in each chapter to create the movie. In the course of following the steps, the reader will learn many techniques and develop skills necessary to do original work. All of the movies featured in this book are also included on the CD.

Hardware and Software Considerations

As with most programs, Flash 5 has some hardware and operating system requirements.

Windows

The hardware requirements for Windows machines are as follows:

- An Intel Pentium 133MHz or better; 200MHz preferred
- 32MB RAM (random access memory); 64MB preferred
- 40MB hard drive space for the Flash programs
- A monitor that will display 800-by-600 pixels resolution
- A CD-ROM drive

Flash 5 will run on Windows 95, Windows 98, Windows NT, Windows 2000, and Windows ME.

Macintosh

Flash 5 has the following hardware requirements on the Macintosh:

- A Macintosh G3 or higher
- 32MB RAM (random access memory); 64MB preferred
- 40MB hard drive space for the Flash programs

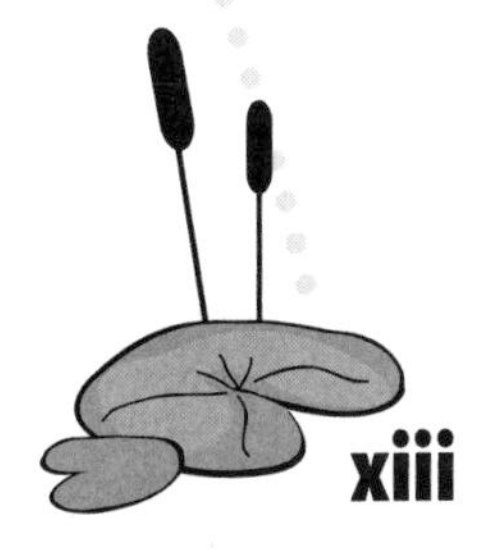

- A monitor that will display 800-by-600 pixels resolution
- A CD-ROM drive

In addition, Flash 5 will run on System 8.5 or later.

How This Book Is Organized

Flash 5 Visual JumpStart leads the reader through a series of progressively more difficult and sophisticated projects. The projects in the book cover most of the tools and techniques needed to create killer Web graphics, sound, and animation.

Here's a brief chapter-by-chapter rundown of what you can expect:

- In Chapters 1 and 2, you will get a tour of the tools and menus and learn how to use them effectively. In both chapters, you'll do some exercises that will give you experience using the tools in the Toolbox along with the tool modifiers and options. An introduction to each of the menus is provided and a section of Chapter 2 details the process of setting preferences for tools, drawing, and the Clipboard.
- Chapter 3 provides instruction in drawing and painting tools and techniques. Types of color are introduced, as well as how to use lines and fill.
- Chapter 4 deals with the creation of symbols and the use of instances of symbols.
- Chapter 5 shows you how to use text creatively and usefully.
- Chapter 6 covers the use of layers. Here, the project is creating a Christmas tree with lights and decorations on separate layers.
- Chapter 7 takes the project from Chapter 6 a step further by working with timelines. The layers of the Christmas tree are animated.
- In Chapters 8 and 9, you'll create a movie in which Max and Sasha (those loveable rottweilers) travel to Mars. In these exercises, you will learn how to create animation and sound—to make a real movie.
- Chapter 10 shows you how to publish your work and upload it to the Web.

The tasks in each chapter are organized so that each moves you a level higher in understanding how to make creative Web sites.

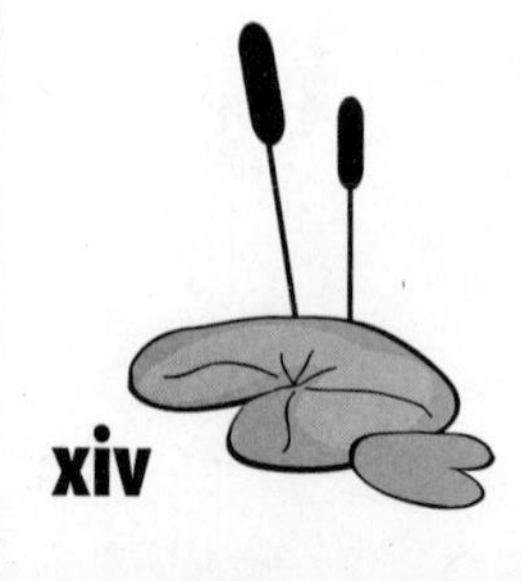

Making the Most of This Book

In each chapter of *Flash 5 Visual JumpStart* you will find a list of topics that you will learn in that chapter.

To enhance your knowledge of Flash and Web design and animation, there are terms that are highlighted in the text and also defined in the margins of the book. Text that you are asked to type will appear in **bold font**. *Italics* indicates words as words and letters as letters. `Monospaced` font displays file and folder names, as well as Internet addresses.

You will also find other elements in the text to help you:

Note

Notes provide extra information and references to related information.

Tip

Tips are insights that help you perform tasks more easily and effectively.

Warning

Warnings let you know about things you should do, or shouldn't do.

Finally, when an operation requires a series of choices from menus or dialog boxes, the ➢ symbol is used to guide you through the instructions, like this: "Select Programs ➢ Accessories ➢ System Tools ➢ System Information." The items the ➢ symbol separates may be menu items, toolbar icons, check boxes, or other elements of the Windows interface—any place you can make a selection.

What's on the CD?

The CD contains all of the Flash authoring files and executable files that have been created over the course of this book. In addition, there are links to many Flash Web sites and some additional programs to peruse.

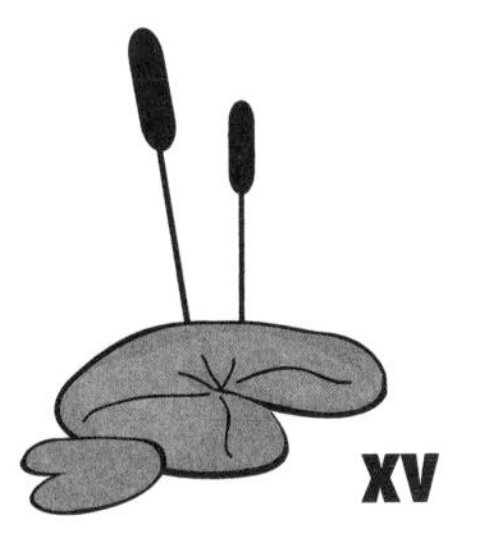

Other Resources

Here is a list of other resources you might find useful:

www.macromedia.com It almost goes without saying that you should check out the Macromedia site.

www.xdude.com The Web site of Digital Dude has links to many other Flash sites. In addition, www.xdude.com/faqs/tips.htm offers help in learning Flash.

www.uistudios.com Offers Flash games, a Flash gallery, and a Flash tutorial.

www.extremeflash.com Extreme Flash displays tutorials that you can download.

www.canfieldstudios.com Canfield Studios supplies some valuable tutorials.

www.flashchallenge.com Offers links to Web design, commercial, and game sites.

www.flashplanet.com Offers cool movies from a Flash contest to celebrate the millennium as well as many other links.

How to Reach the Author

Patricia A. Hartman can be reached at patriciahartman@hitekdesigns.com.

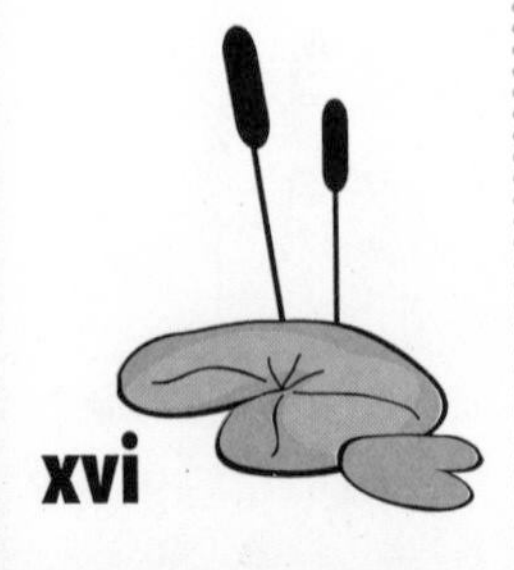

Part 1

Getting into Flash

Before you can start creating in Flash, you need to know where to go to find the right tools. Even though you may have worked in other graphics and web applications, Flash may not be intuitive to you. To begin, you'll take a tour of the Flash interface, explore the menus and tools, and set your Flash preferences to work for you.

Getting into Flash

Chapter 1

Understanding the Flash Interface

The Flash 5 interface provides a work area that operates similarly to a stage with tools and props. This chapter gives you the basics, so that you can jump right in and begin creating great graphics. It is helpful to learn about the Stage, where most of the action takes place, before tackling the tools and their uses. So in this chapter, you'll get a taste of Flash to prepare you for exercises in subsequent chapters.

- Learning About Flash Concepts
- Recognizing the Stage and Its Content
- Becoming Familiar with the Tools

Launching Flash

When you launch Flash, immediately you'll see a window with title bars displaying Movie1, Scene 1, and Layer 1. This is the default for a new movie. Movies are what Flash does. Although it is easy to create motionless graphics in Flash, most of what you will do will in some way be animated. For example, a menu might not be a movie in the usual sense, but the menu items could be presented so that they change color and size depending upon the position of the cursor. In this sense, then, a menu would be a movie.

To start a new movie in Flash, follow these steps:

1. Launch Flash. A blank Flash scene will appear; the first example is on a Windows machine and the second is on a Mac.

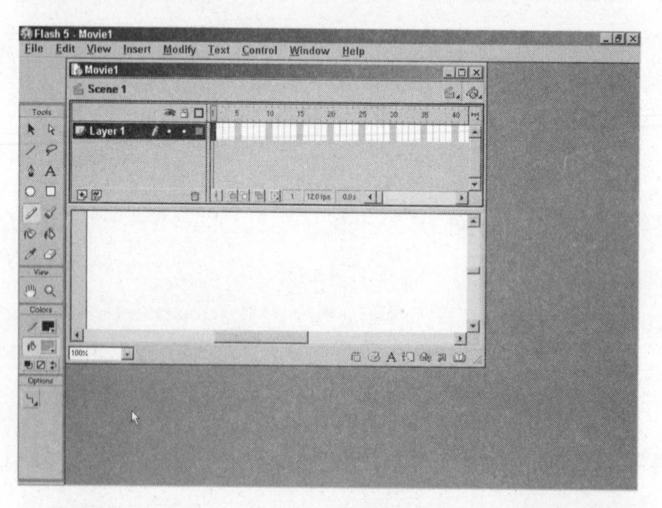

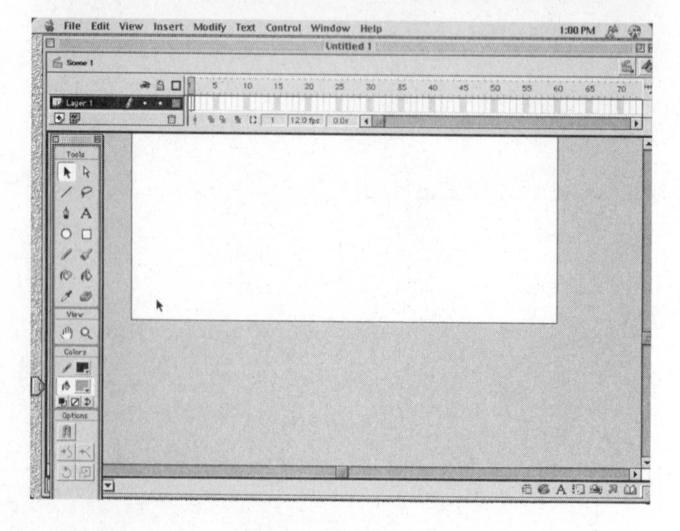

2. To create a new file, select File ➢ New.

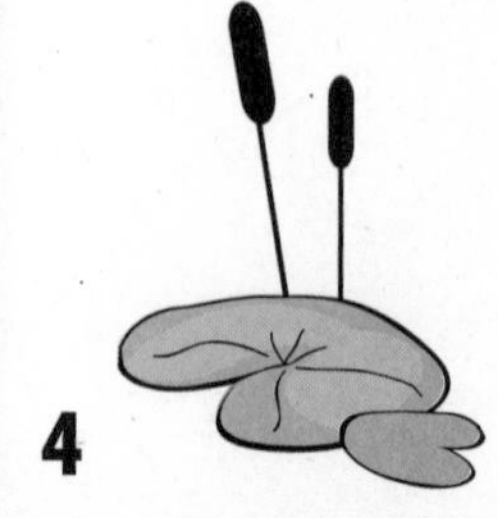

Recognizing the Stage and Its Content

Located approximately at the bottom half of the screen is a large blank area. This is the Stage. This is where you will position and assemble the parts of the movie you are working on. Directly under the toolbar is the title bar for the scene. You can create movies with more than one scene, just as you can motion pictures and plays. Go ahead and save the movie by clicking the disk icon on the toolbar or by selecting Save from the File menu. Even though you haven't done anything yet, you will now have a movie file that you can work on.

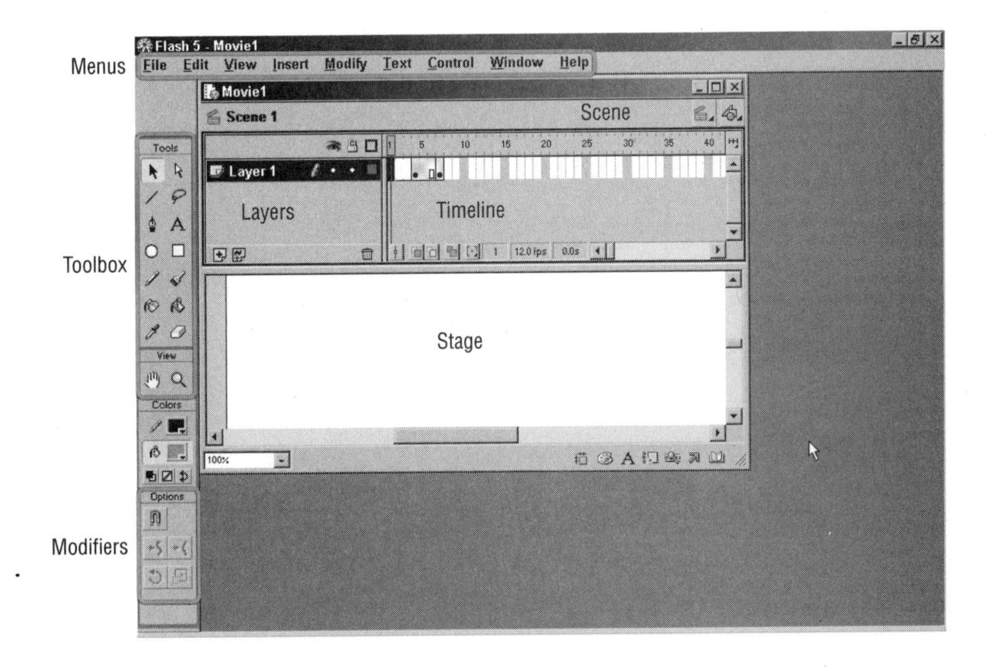

Creating a Layer

Under the scene title bar is the Layer area. Layers are important because they separate graphics within the same scene. A scene can have many layers. Ideally, you should name each layer differently to reflect its nature or what it does in the scene. For example, you could name a layer "box" if it contains a moving box.

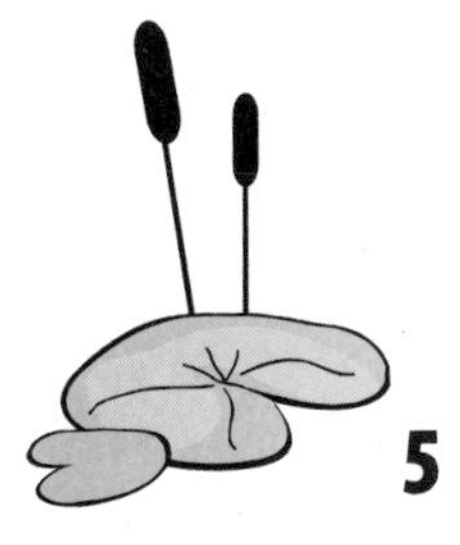

To create a layer, follow these steps:

1. Click the Insert Layer icon (the plus sign) in the lower-left corner of the Layer pane. Now you have a new layer.
2. After viewing the new layer, select Layer 2 and click the trash can icon in the lower-right corner of the Layer pane to delete the new layer.

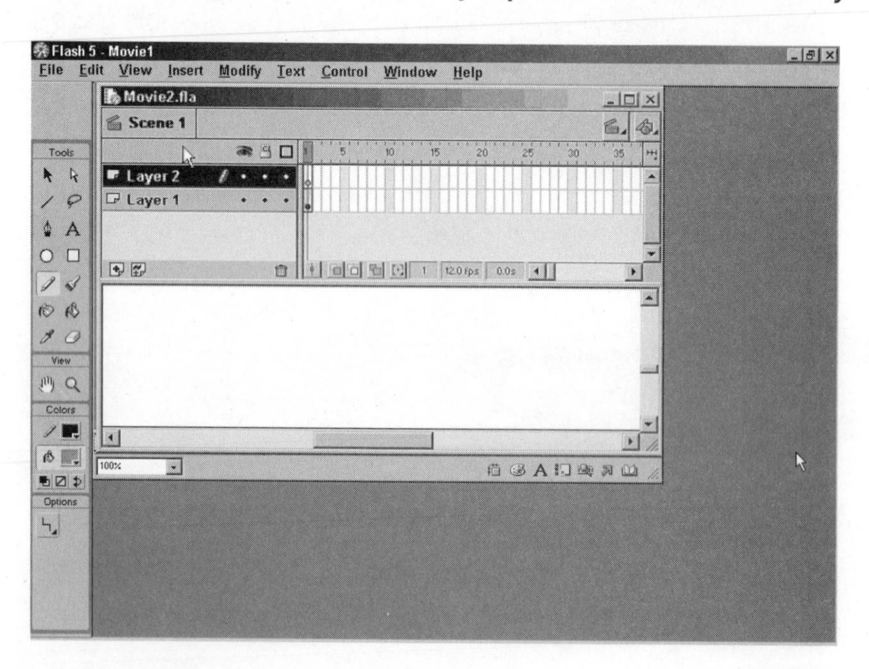

Understanding the Timeline

In the right pane of the Layer area is what appears to be a ruler with numbers incremented at regular intervals. This is the **timeline**. It can be broken into a series of points (called **frames**) in which some activity or change from previous activity takes place.

timeline
A timeline represents the chronological order of frames in a movie.

frame
A frame is the smallest unit of change in an object or symbol on the timelines of a movie. In films, a frame is one of numerous still shots that, when put together, create action. Static frames maintain action or content from previous frames. Keyframes are points of change.

Tip

Each layer can have its own timeline and each timeline can have frames, which are marked points on the timeline.

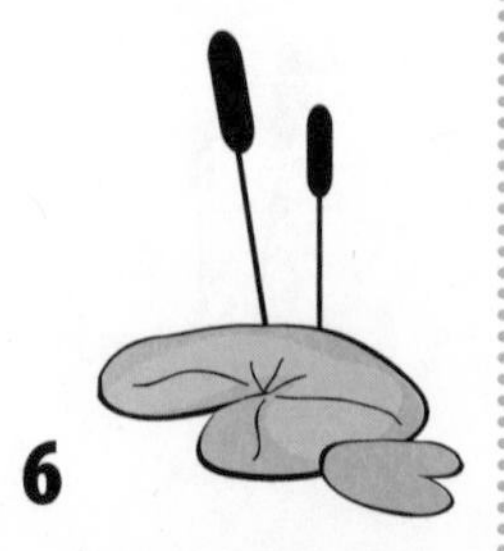

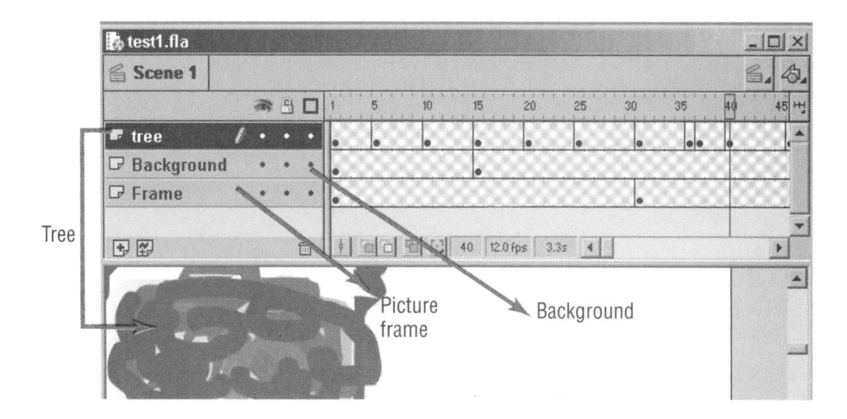

Working with Frames

Perhaps you have previously created animated GIF files by saving a group of bitmap files in a movie format. If this is the case, then you are well aware of the large amount of work that an exercise with frames requires. If you have ever slowed a videotape to view each frame separately, you will realize that movies are made up of many frames that cause action to appear to take place when they are viewed in quick succession. Before motion pictures, an example of the frame concept consisted of a group of cards on which symbols or pictures were drawn in sequence, with each picture drawn slightly differently. When the cards were shuffled or flipped quickly, the drawings blurred together to make a primitive kind of movie. You will be glad to know that Flash will automate this process for you.

To begin working with frames, follow these steps:

1. In the document you've been working in, select the layer labeled Layer 1.
2. Move the cursor to the timeline and right-click (Ctrl+click on the Mac) anywhere on the timeline.
3. Select Insert Frame to insert a frame on the timeline.

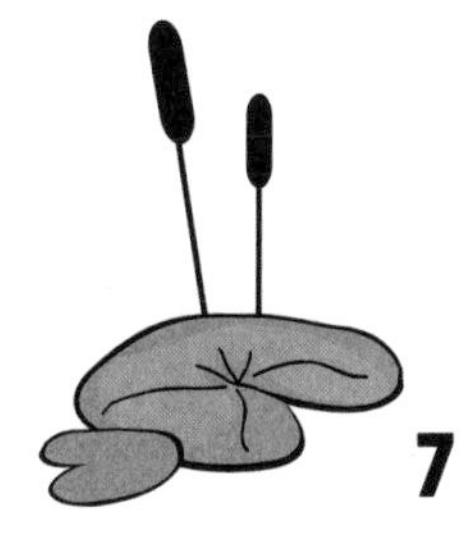

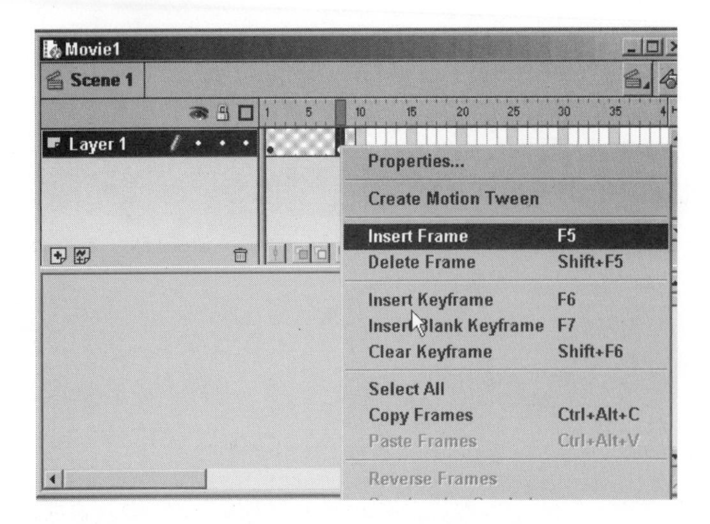

4. Move the cursor five points to the right of the new frame, then right-click again to insert another frame.

5. Notice that the timeline area in which frames have been inserted changes in appearance so that the vertical lines seem to fade out, leaving a blank area.

6. Click anywhere inside the area in which you have inserted a frame. This will produce a red vertical line on the timeline.

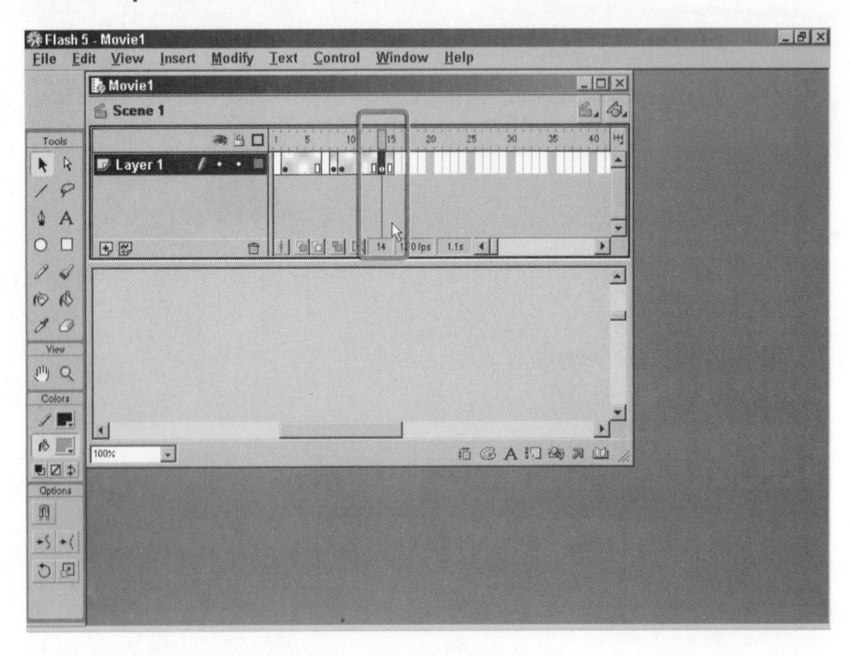

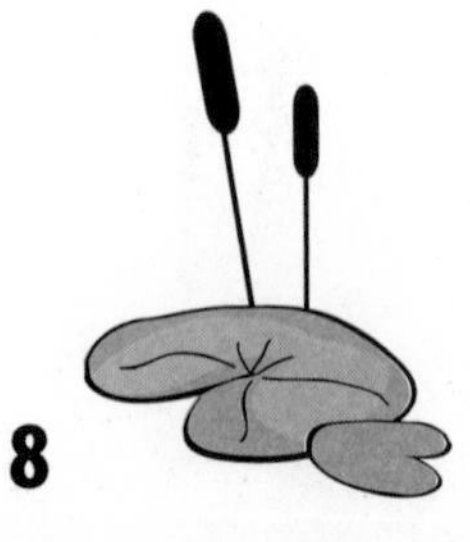

7. Click along the timeline to the right of the area where you inserted frames. You will not see a red line.

Note

The changed appearance of the timeline indicates that frames have been inserted. The red line indicates a selected frame.

Placing an Object on the Stage

When you place an **object** on the **Stage**, you can control where it displays, how long it is displayed, and what color or shape it is during the scene. You determine these factors by your placement of frames at specific intervals on the points of the timeline for the current layer. Let's try it:

object
A line, shape, drawing, text, imported graphic, audio file, or video clip.

Stage
The work area on which a movie is built.

1. Remove any frames you have inserted, except for the frame at the position numbered 1. Do this by right-clicking (Ctrl+click on the Mac) on the frame and selecting Remove Frames.

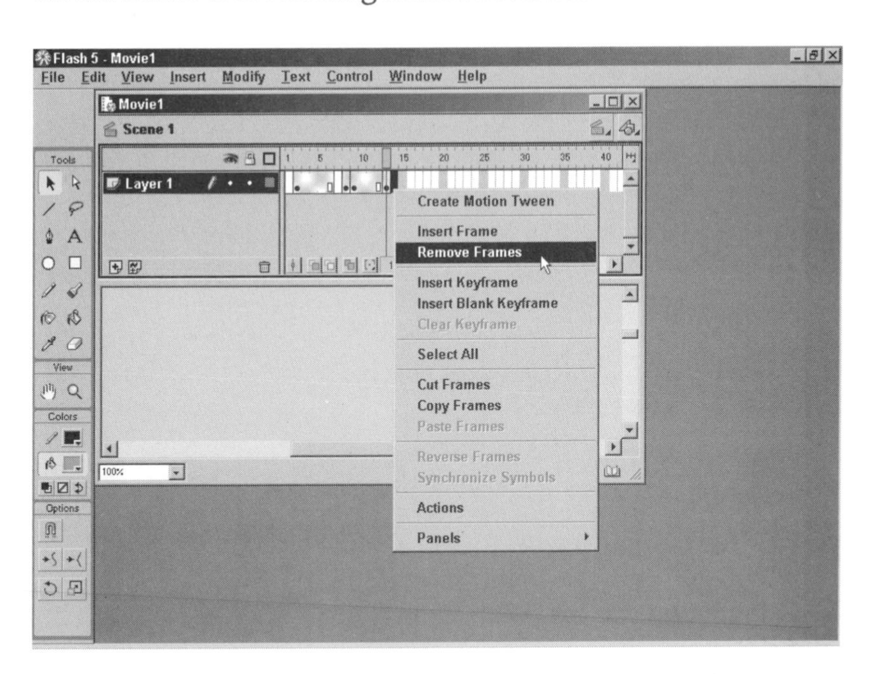

2. Click the Rectangle tool (the square icon in the right column of the Toolbox, under the letter *A*).

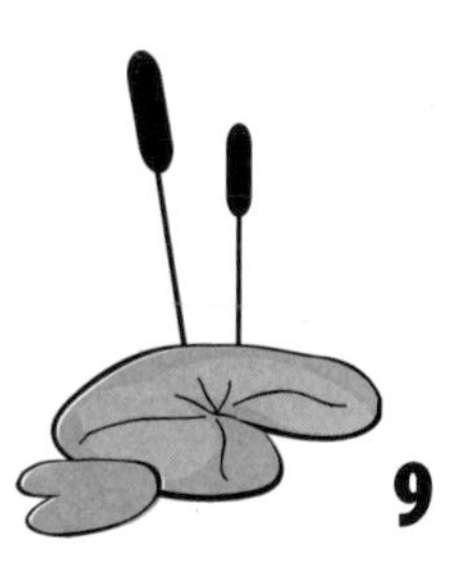

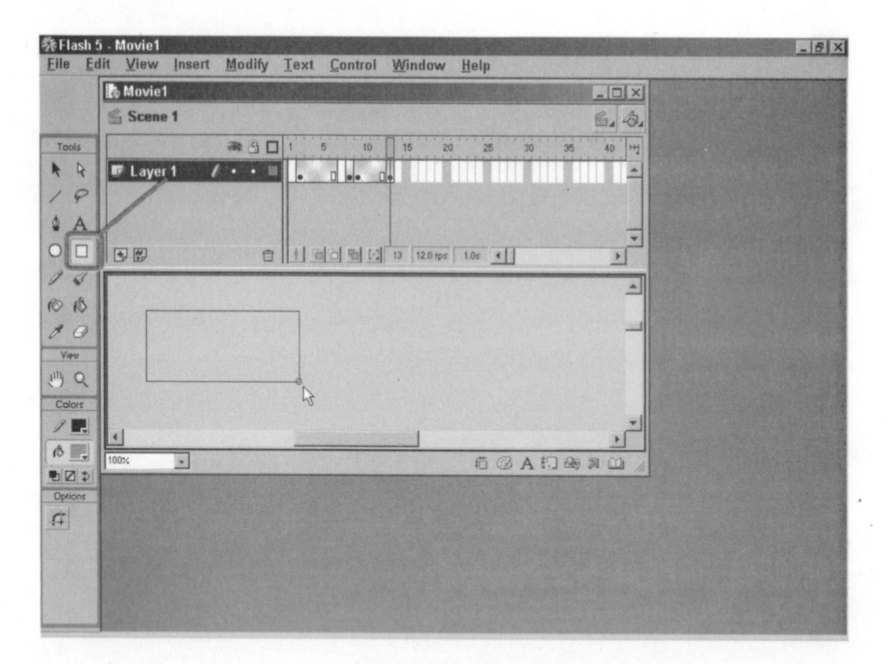

3. Next, click in the upper-left corner of the Stage, and while holding the left mouse button down, drag toward the lower right for about two or three inches until you have drawn a rectangle. Release the mouse button.

Tip

If you have not previously used one, you may need to practice clicking and dragging the mouse. You can do this by moving the mouse while continuing to hold down the left button. Do this in the Stage area. Don't worry if you make a mistake. You can select Edit ➢ Undo to remove your last change or begin again by clicking the New icon, pressing Ctrl+N, or selecting New from the File menu.

4. The rectangle will be attached to the frame that was selected when you drew the rectangle.

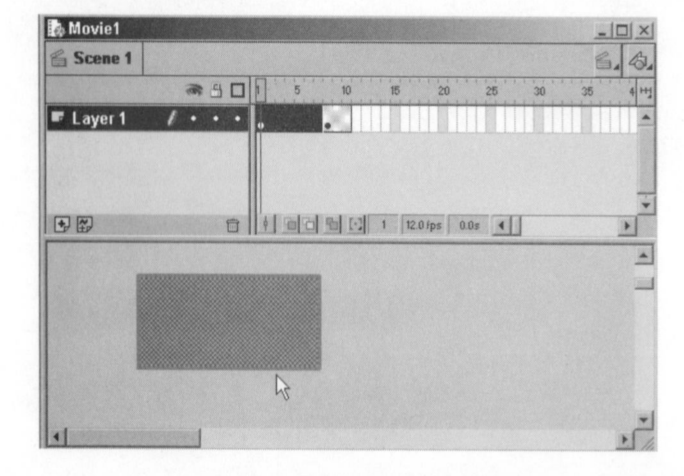

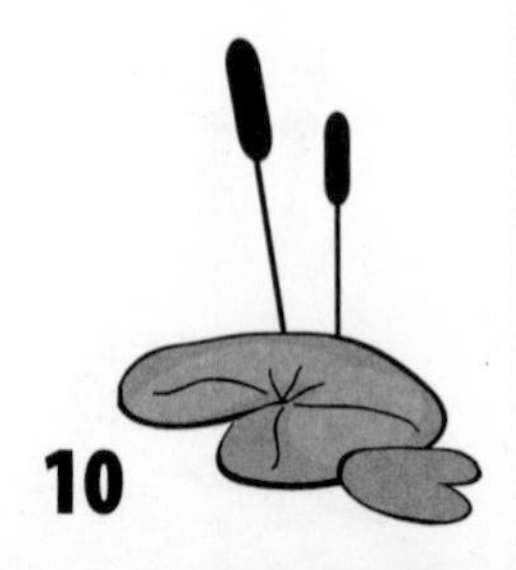

Using Keyframes

There is a special kind of frame called **keyframe**. When you associate a change in an object with a new frame, the frame must be a keyframe.

keyframe
A frame that marks a change in an object's properties from the preceding frame. When you associate the change in an object with the new frame, the frame is then a keyframe. The first frame on the timeline must be a keyframe.

Tip

There are static frames and keyframes. Static frames maintain only the contents of a previous frame. Changes in action must be attached to keyframes.

You can devise a new action for your object to take after it moves along the timeline to a keyframe; when the timeline reaches the keyframe, the change or start of a new activity takes place. Here's how to associate an action to a keyframe:

1. Select a keyframe by first selecting a frame on one of the layers and then right-clicking (Ctrl+click on the Mac) and selecting Insert Keyframe from the context menu.

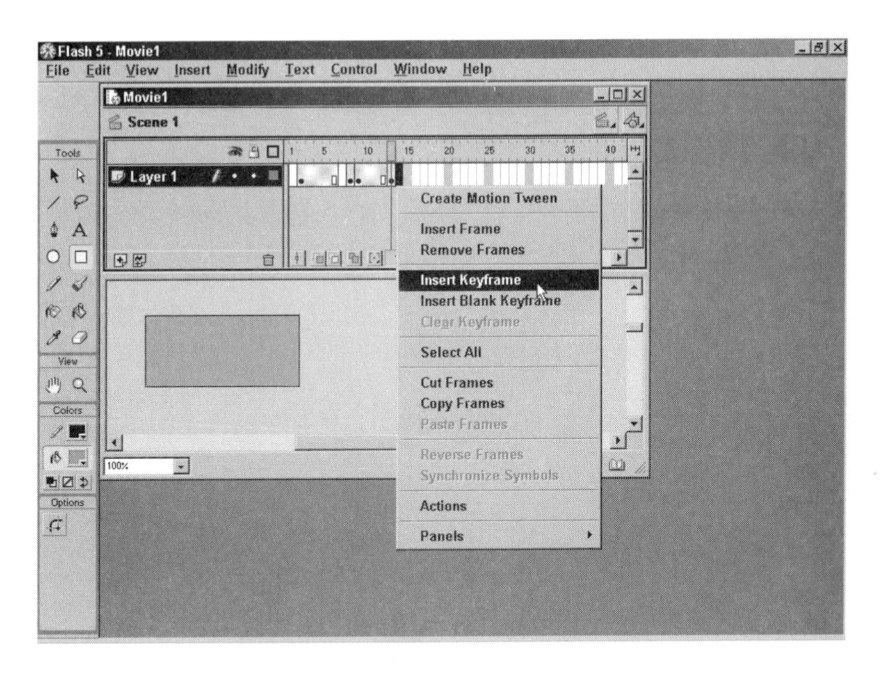

2. Move the rectangle to a different position with the keyframe selected.

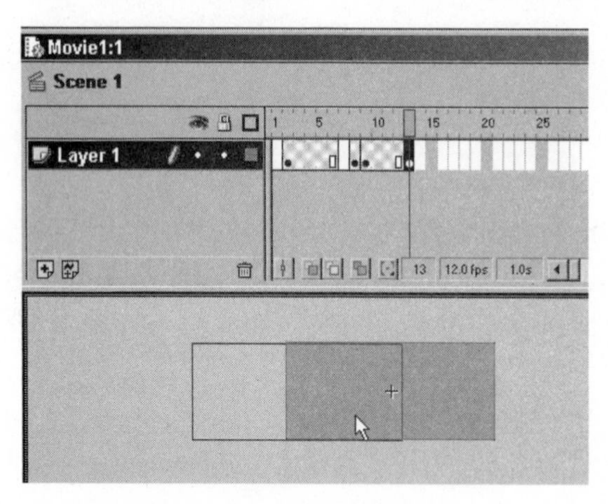

Moving the Object

Objects that you place on the Stage can be controlled by the position of the frames on the timeline. For example, while a frame is selected, you can move an object to a new position and change its color and shape:

1. Insert a keyframe 5 to 10 points to the right of the first frame (the left-most frame).
2. Click the Arrow tool, then select the rectangle by drawing a box around it (click and drag just as you did to draw the rectangle, but draw outside the rectangle so that it is selected).

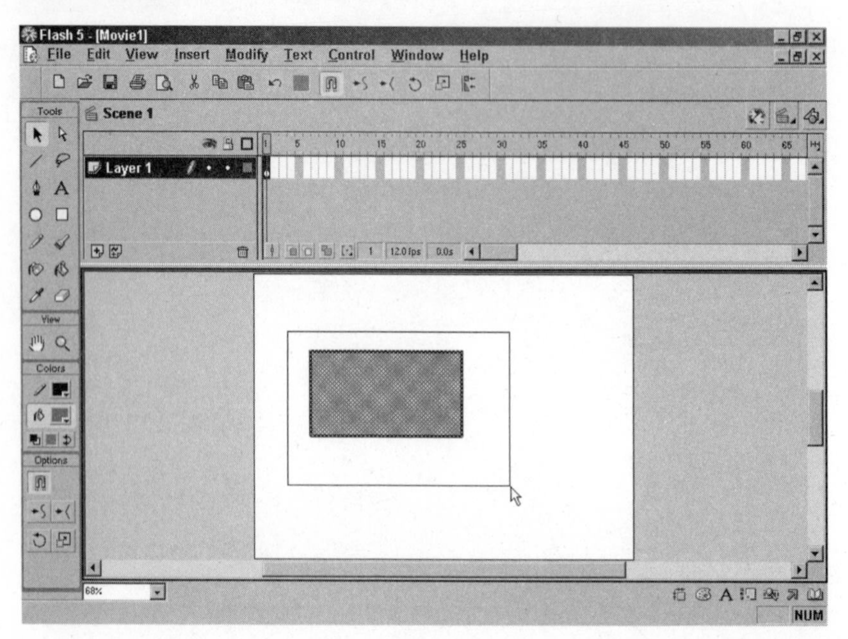

3. When the rectangle is selected, it will change color so that it appears to be crosshatched or grayed out. You can then move it without leaving the outline behind.

Tip

If a box's outline becomes separated from the fill when you try to drag it, you can delete it and start over. Select the individual parts and press the Delete key until the box has been removed from the stage, or you can select the entire object and then press the Delete key only once. You also can use Edit ➢ Undo to roll the scene back to the state it was in prior to your mistake.

4. With the new frame selected (the red line is visible), click and drag the selected box. Drag it a small distance from where you started.

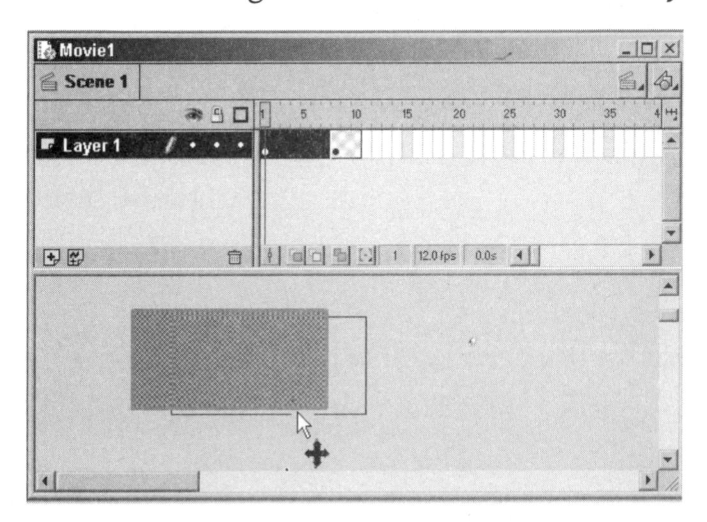

5. When you finish, you should be able to click the frame point and see the box jump between the two frames you have inserted.

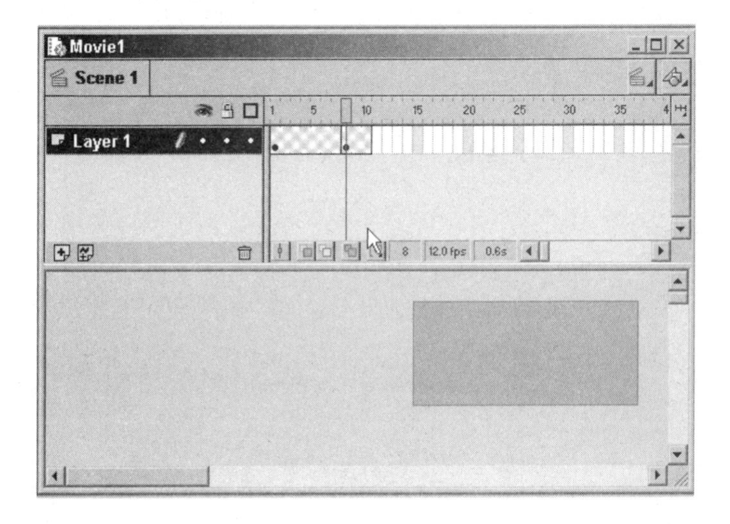

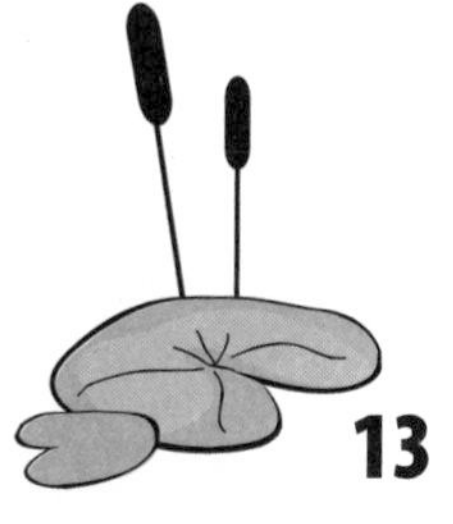

Note

Keep in mind that there is a lot going on all at once in Flash. You can have multiple layers, each with its own timeline and many frames on the timeline. In addition, you can have a number of objects on the stage, each with its own scenario of appearances in different layers and points on the timeline. And this is within one scene. Besides all that, you can import sound and graphics from other programs and individual files. The Flash movie is based upon the set of instructions you create to carry out the scenario you design.

Creating a Symbol

symbol
Symbols are reusable objects.

As rewarding as it is to draw objects on the Stage, it is not really very efficient to create all your objects from scratch. In fact, your creations can be more easily manipulated when they become **symbols**. When you create symbols, you can modify instances of the symbols without changing the symbols themselves. Let's create a symbol so you can reuse it repeatedly without modifying the original artwork:

1. Select the rectangle again and choose Convert to Symbol from the Insert menu.
2. In the Symbol Properties dialog box, type the name, **rectangle**. Set the Behavior option to Graphic and click OK.

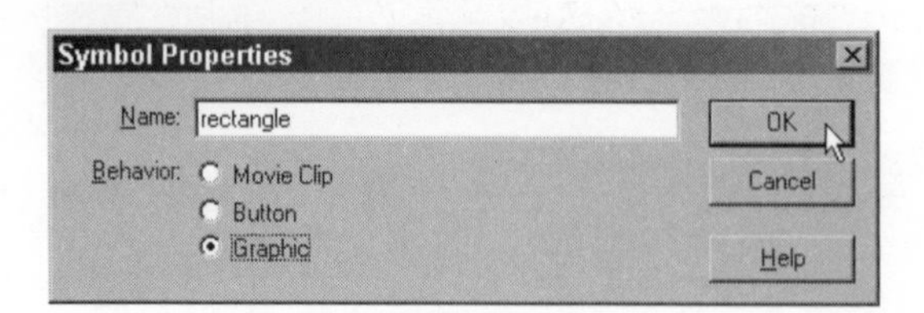

instance
Instances are different occurrences of symbols. Instances can be changed without changing the original symbol or object. For example, if you wanted to depict an army, you could create one soldier, convert it to a symbol, and then copy instances of it, modifying the instances so they are slightly different from one another. This greatly simplifies making movies with numerous objects.

Creating an Instance

Now let's create an **instance** of the rectangle symbol. Instances, which are copies of a symbol, can be changed into different versions and placed at various points along the timeline. If you converted a circle to a symbol, you would

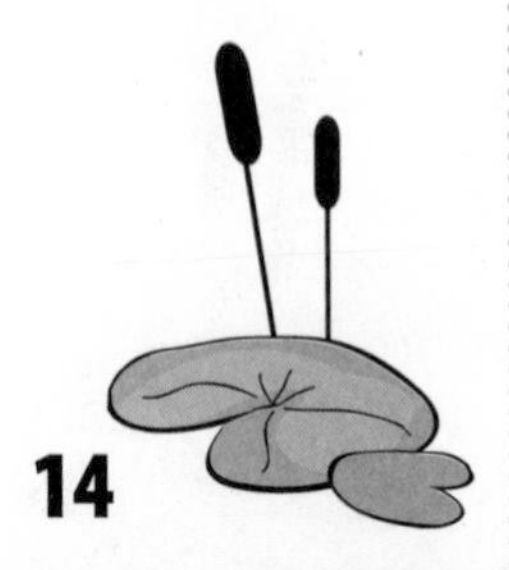

be able to change the size and color of an instance of that symbol without changing the original.

Here's how to create an instance of the rectangle symbol:

1. Select Modify ➢ Instance.
2. Select the Instance tab.
3. Select Graphic from the drop-down list next to the Behavior option and select Loop from the list below the Behavior drop-down menu.

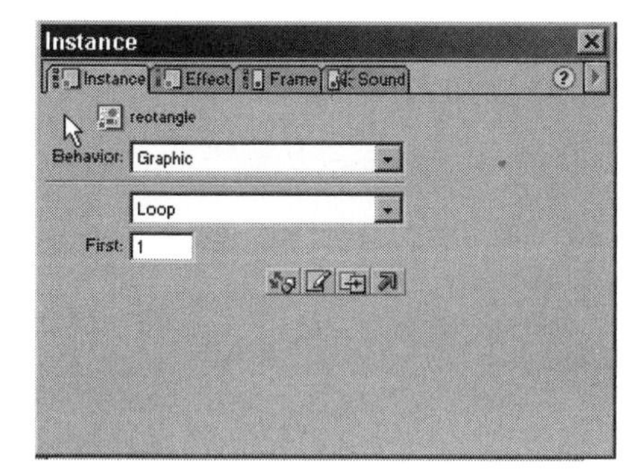

Viewing the Library

Whenever you open a Flash movie file (`myfile.fla`), you will also have access to the library that accompanies it. You can view the **Library** window by selecting Library from the Window menu.

Library
The feature that stores, organizes, and displays symbols, bitmaps, sound files, and videos.

Note

When you create objects and modify their attributes, they can be converted to symbols and appear in the Library.

Imported files also will be included in the Library. The Library of symbols is typically always available with a movie. You can view the symbol in the upper pane of the Library window by selecting the text name in the lower pane:

1. Select Window ➢ Library.

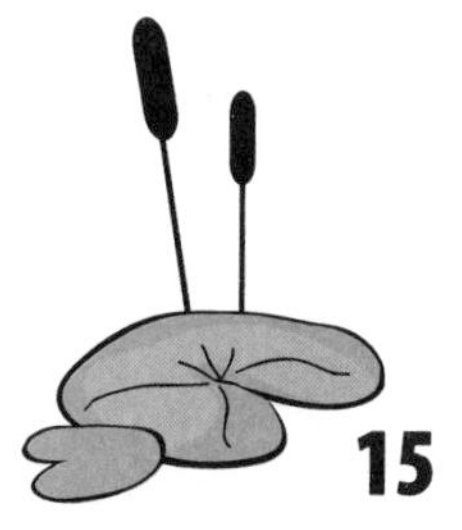

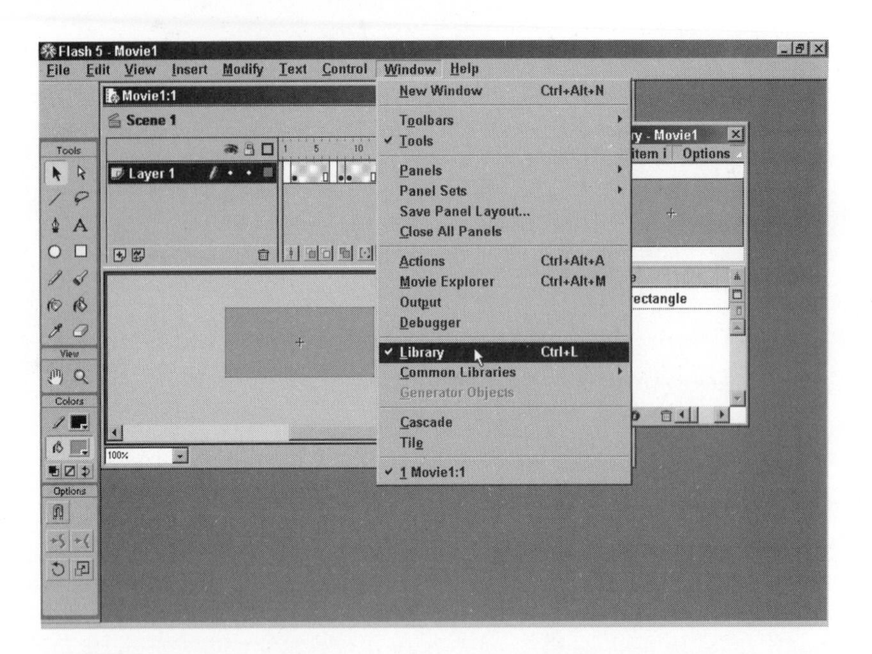

2. Click the name rectangle in the Name pane of the Library window.

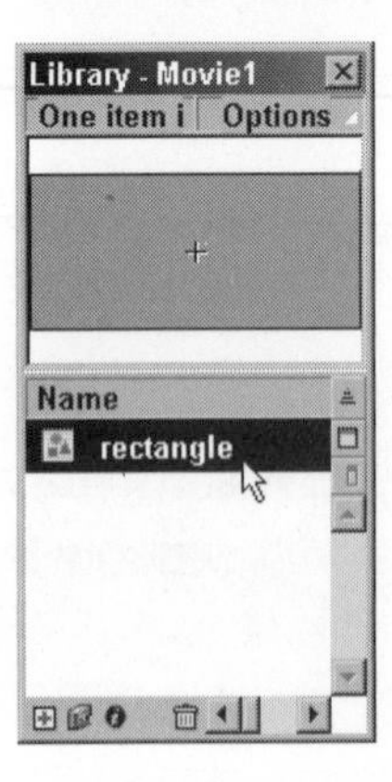

3. View the rectangle in the upper pane of the Library window.

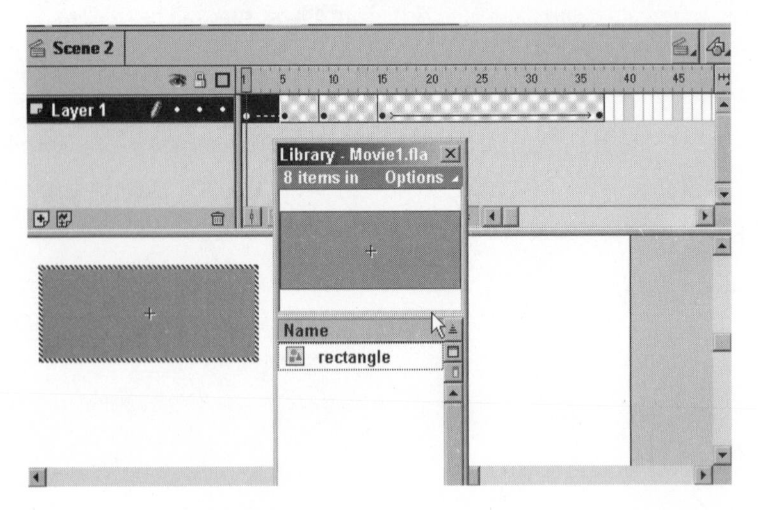

4. If you create a number of symbols, their names display on a list in the Name pane of the Library window. Selecting the name of the symbol will cause the graphic to be displayed in the top half of the Library window.

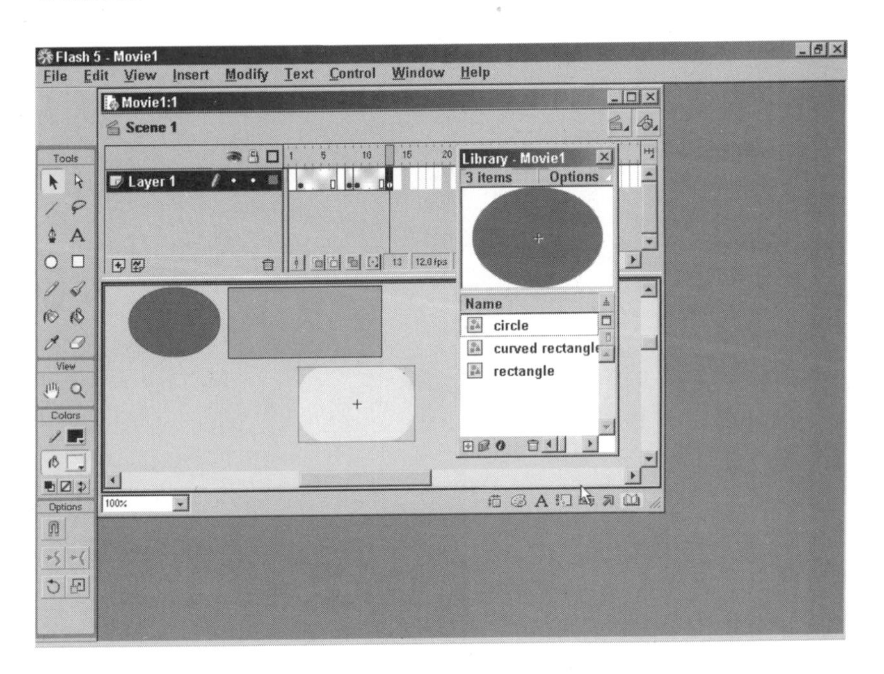

Becoming Familiar with Flash's Tools

So far, you have used several of the Flash tools—the Arrow (selection) tool and the Rectangle tool—as well as selected options from several menus. Still, you have not yet scratched the surface of all the wonderful features contained in Flash.

Tip

You can view the name of the tool each icon represents by moving the mouse cursor over the icon and pausing to see the tooltip. When the cursor is passed over the icon, a small box (tooltip) will pop up displaying the name of the tool as well as the keyboard shortcut associated with it.

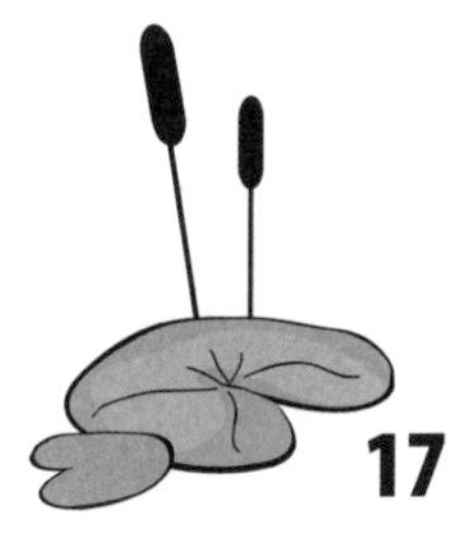

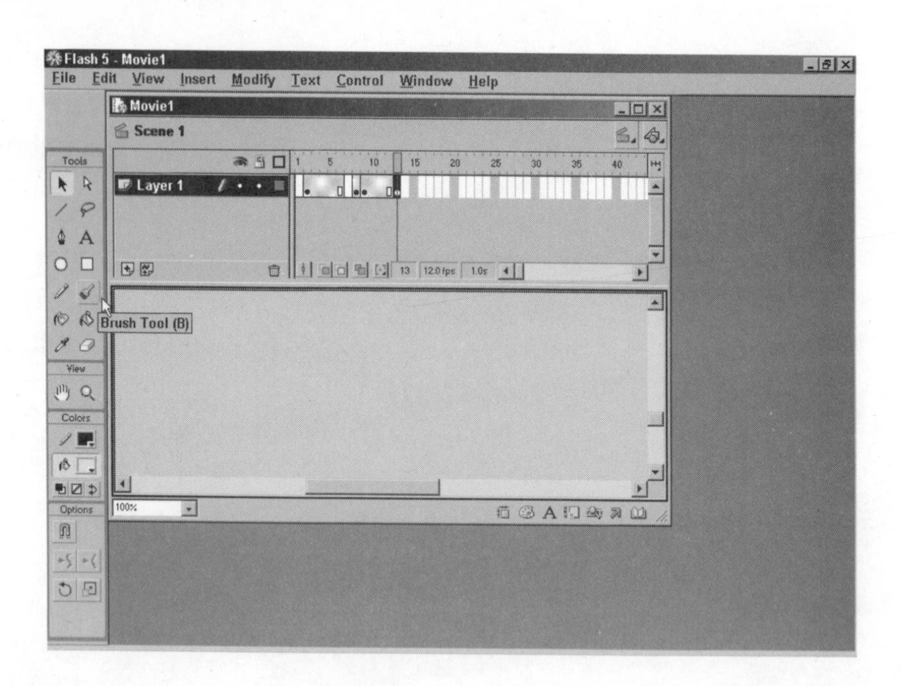

The Toolbar

toolbar

The set of icons at the top of the screen immediately under the menu bar. The Mac does not have a toolbar.

If you don't see the Flash **toolbar**, you can view it by selecting Window ➢ Toolbars ➢ Main.

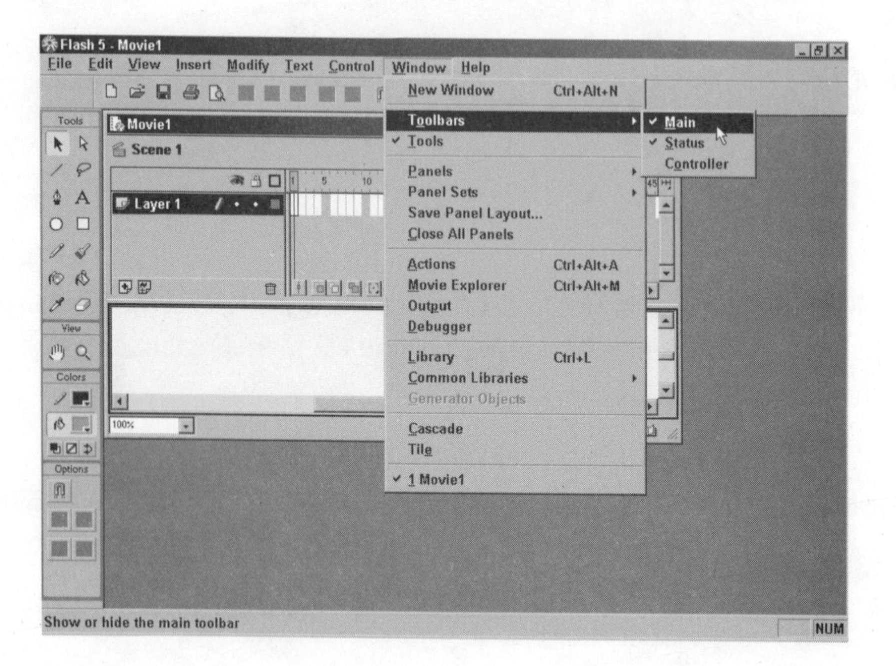

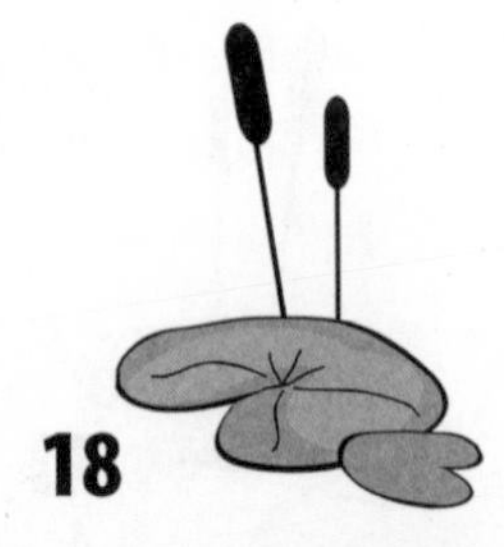

These icons are typical of most Windows programs; you can use them to create a new file, open a file, save a file, print, zoom, cut, copy, and paste. However, Flash adds some tools here to undo, redo, snap, smooth, straighten, rotate, scale, and align. These Flash-specific tools are also available from the menus.

Tip

The toolbar (with its mostly generic tools) is different than the Toolbox, which contains the Flash drawing, painting, and text tools.

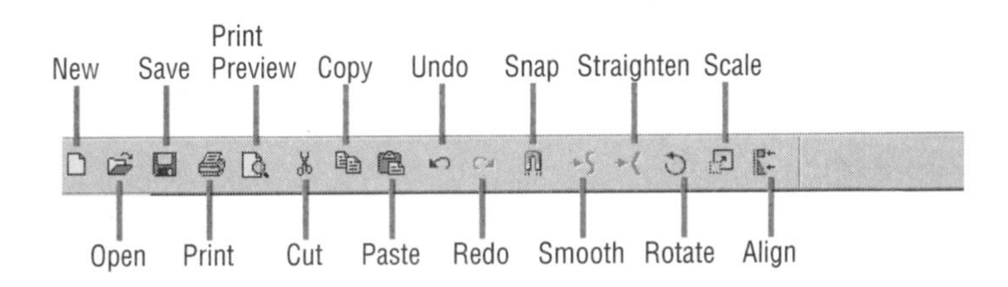

Note

Macintosh applications do not provide toolbars; you can access these tools from the menus.

The tools carry out the following commands:

New Create a new movie

Open Open a movie file

Save Save a movie

Print Print objects on the Stage

Print Preview Preview objects before printing

Cut Cut the current selection

Copy Copy the current selection

Paste Paste from the Clipboard

Undo Remove the last task performed

Redo Reapply the task just undone

Snap Snap to a grid

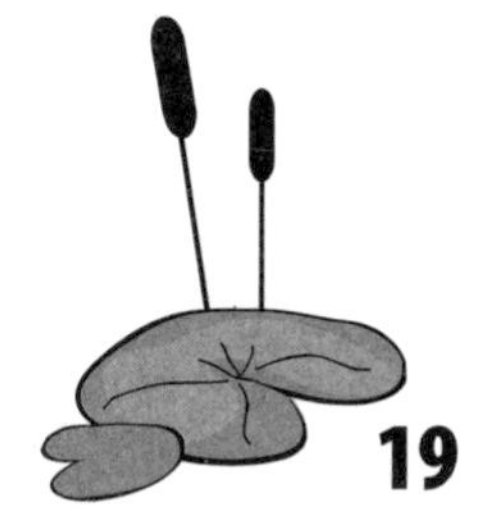

Smooth Smooth a curved line

Straighten Straighten a straight line

Rotate Rotate a selection

Scale Scale an object or group

Align Align selected objects to each other or the stage

Moving and Docking the Toolbar

If you don't like the placement of the toolbar, you can reposition it:

1. Grab the toolbar by clicking and dragging with the mouse. You must grab it by the gray area adjacent to the icons. Do not click an icon or you will initiate that option.
2. Move the toolbar to a part of the screen you find more convenient. The toolbar is now floating.

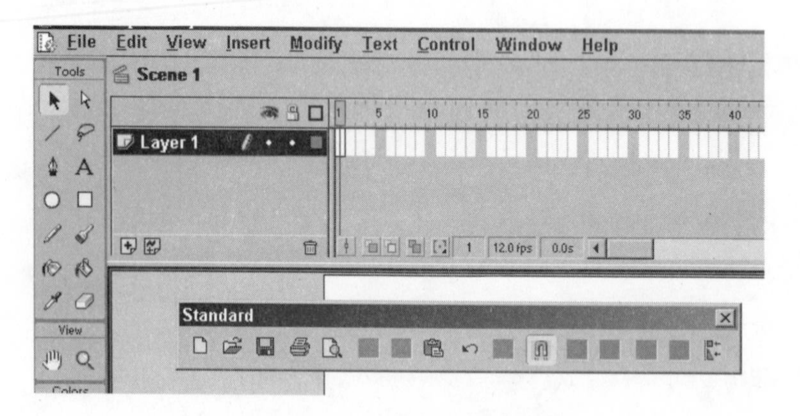

3. Click the title bar of the toolbar and drag it back to its original placement. It will snap back into place. Now it is docked.

The Toolbox

The Toolbox contains the tools you will use to select, create, and modify your images in Flash. It is usually positioned on the upper-left corner of the work area. The Toolbox is sometimes called the drawing toolbar because its tools

enable you to draw, paint, and write. In other words, you can draw with the Toolbox tools, but most of the toolbar tools are generic and work like those in other programs.

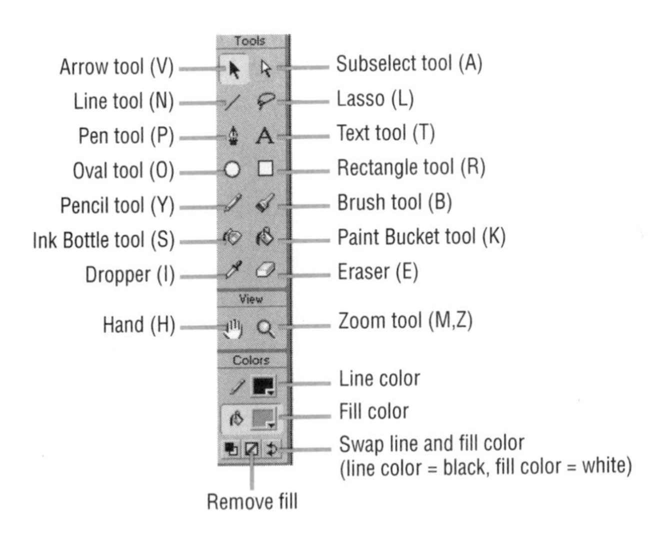

Working with the Tool Options and Panels

For each of the tools in the Toolbox, there is a set of tool options. These options are displayed immediately under the Toolbox.

Note

Although the top of the Toolbox remains the same, the options at the bottom of the Toolbox change depending upon the currently selected tool.

Tool panels provide more options to use with the Toolbox tools. You can use them by selecting Window ➢ Panels. You also can select Panel Sets, which will give you the default layout to modify most tools. (Chapter 2 covers how to use the panels in Flash.)

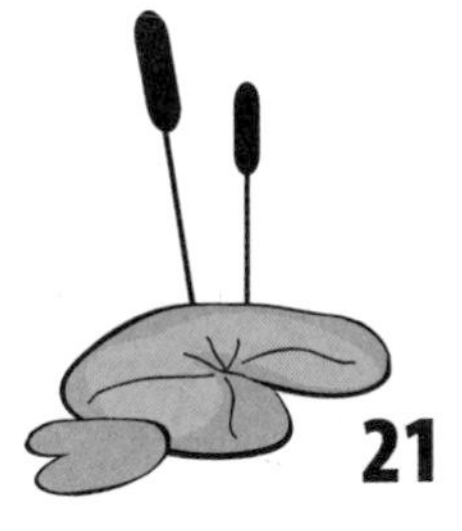

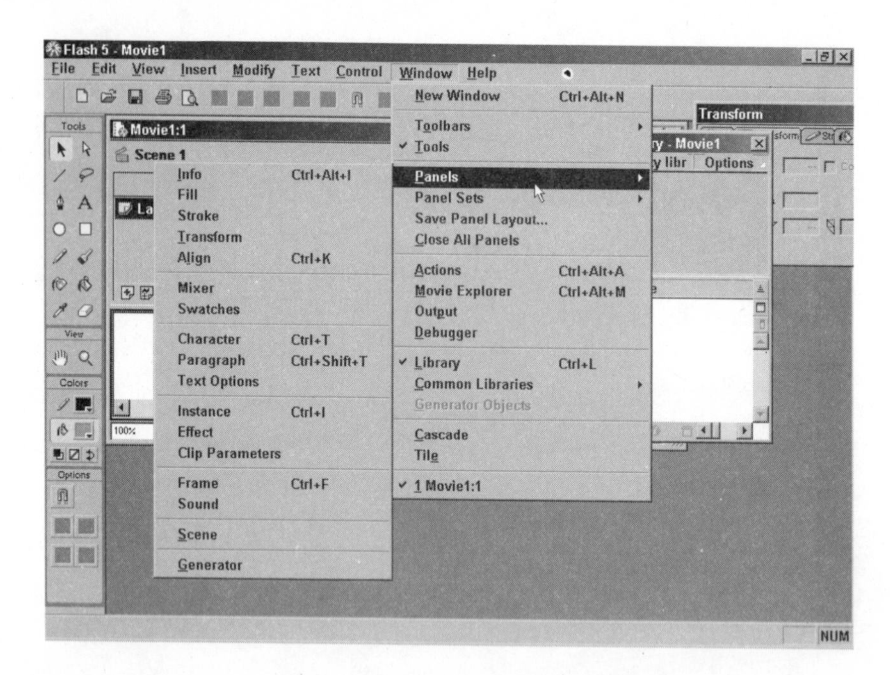

For your convenience, the following table includes brief explanations of the tools and their options.

Tool	Option	Purpose
Pencil	Straighten, Smooth, Ink	Draws free-form lines that can be modified by options. Use as you would a real pencil.
Text	Character, Paragraph and Static, Dynamic, or Input	Places text blocks on the stage. Round handles denote blocks with expanding width, and square handles indicate those with fixed width.
Brush	Paint Normal, Paint Fills, Paint Selection, Paint Behind, Paint Inside, Brush Size, and Shape.	Paints area with brush strokes, depending upon option chosen, using fill color selected.
Eraser	Faucet Modifier, Erase Fills, Lines, Erase Selected Fills, Erase Inside, Brush Size, and Shape.	Erases fills and strokes. Can be customized to erase only selected areas, line segments, fills inside lines, etc.
Arrow	Snap	Toggles Snap to Grid and connection lines on and off.
	Smooth	Smoothes the selected lines.

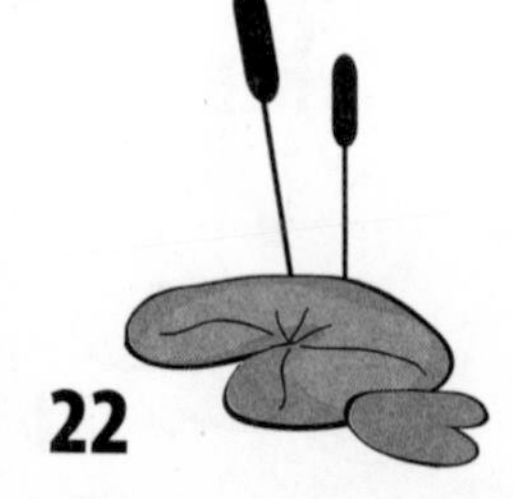

Tool	Option	Purpose
Arrow	Straighten	Straightens the selected lines.
	Rotate	Displays rotation handles for movement.
	Scale	Displays scaling handles to change size.
Lasso	Magic Wand	Toggles smart bitmap selection.
	Magic Wand properties	Allows you to edit the properties.
	Polygon Mode	Changes the Lasso to the Polygon mode.
Rectangle	Round Rectangle Radius	Changes the radius of (creates) a round rectangle.
Paint Bucket	Gap Size	Sets the gap size to be closed by the Paint Bucket.

Moving and Docking the Toolbox

As you can with the toolbar, you can dock the Toolbox or allow it to float:

1. Grab the Toolbox by clicking and dragging with the mouse. Grab it by the gray area above the icons. Do not click on an icon or you will select that option.

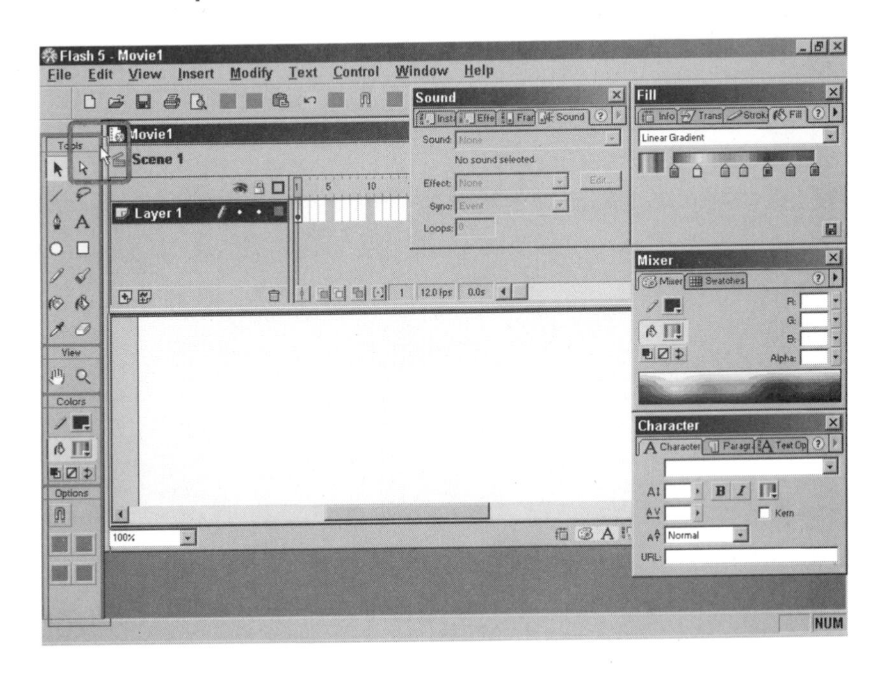

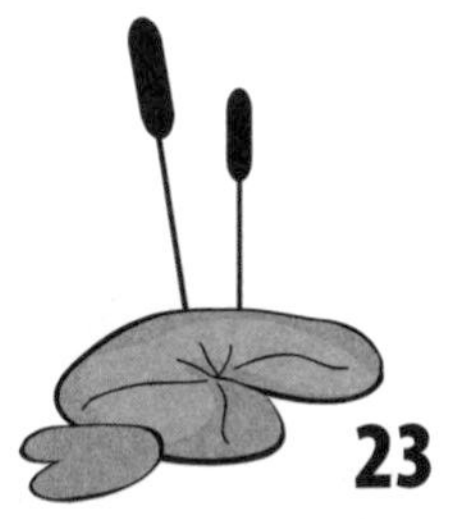

2. Move the Toolbox to a part of the screen you find more convenient. The Toolbox is now floating.

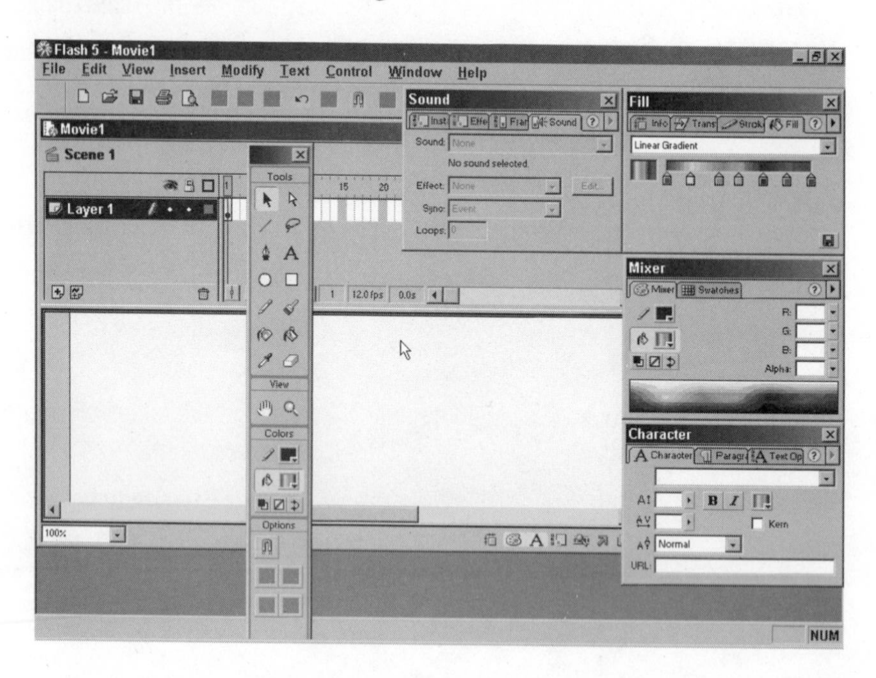

3. Click on the title bar of the Toolbox as you did in step 1 and drag it back to its original placement at the left edge of the screen. It will snap back into place. Now it is docked.

What's Next?

Now that you have practiced using the tools, you are ready to learn about some of the additional features offered by the menu options. There are many dazzling features in Flash. It's easy to get stuck on a particular task when you lack familiarity with the tool you need to use or the properties you need to set. In the next chapter, you'll finish laying the groundwork you need to create great animation for your Web site.

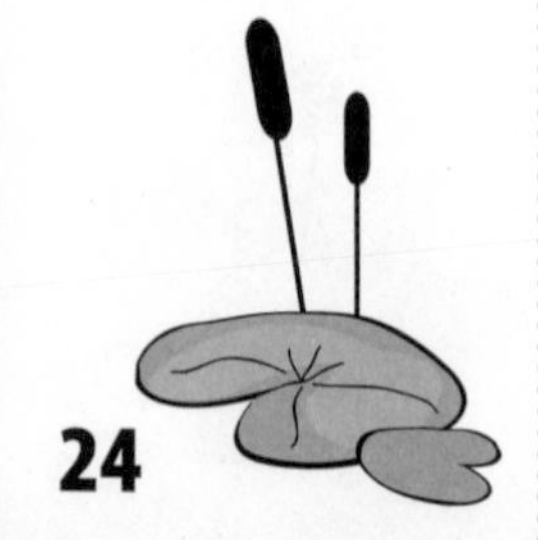

Chapter 2

Mastering Menus and Settings

In Chapter 1, you learned about some of the tools in the Toolbox. In this chapter, you'll learn about some of the useful menu commands and utilities (you were introduced to many of the menu options in the preceding chapter because they also are on the Standard toolbar or associated with the tools). You'll also set up Flash to work efficiently as you tackle the exercises in the rest of the book.

- Explore Tools in the Menu
- Customize Flash Settings

Understanding Menu Options

You may be familiar with the Windows or Macintosh menus from experience with other applications. If so, you will notice that the Flash menus are similar. This quick tour will bring you up to speed on where you can find the tools.

Using File Menu Commands

The File menu contains most of the commands you'll use to open and set up files.

Creating, Opening, and Saving Files

From the File menu, you can create, open, and save files as well as export, import, and publish them:

1. Select File to view the File menu options.

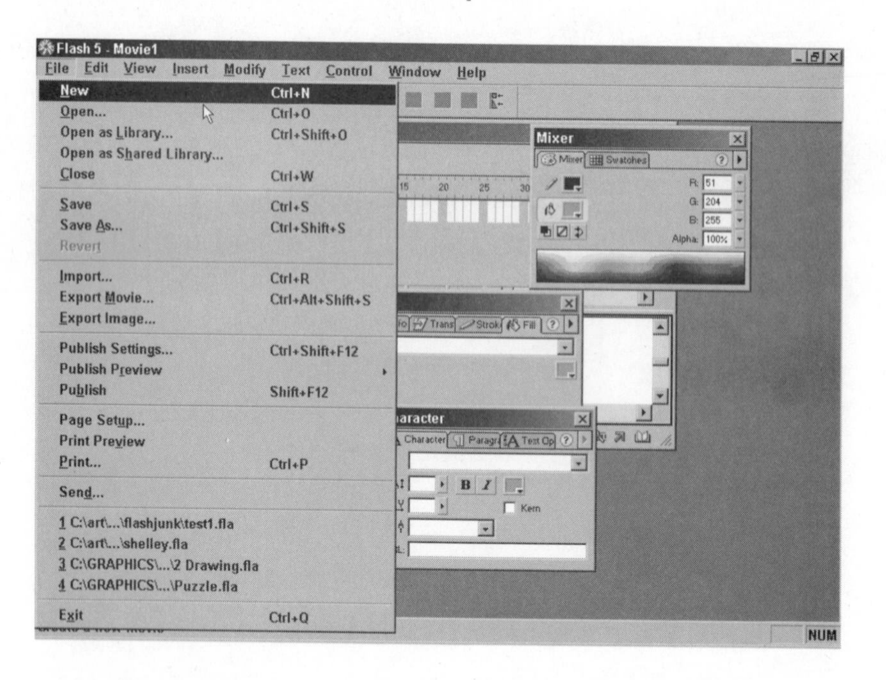

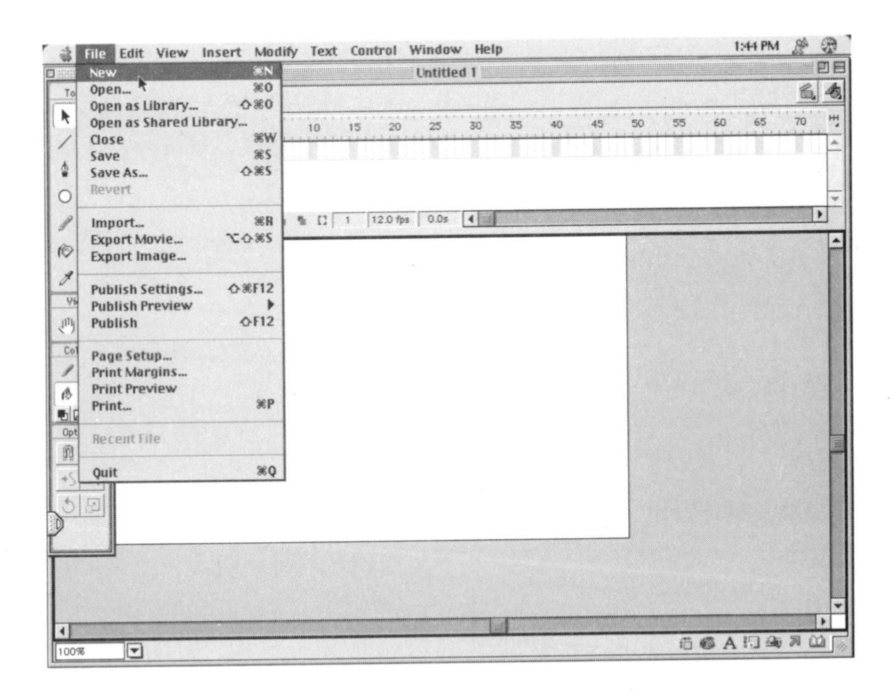

2. Select File ➢ Open. As you can see, the dialog box allows you to select the source folder and filename for the movie you want to open. If you saved the movie you created in Chapter 1, you should be able to locate and retrieve it.

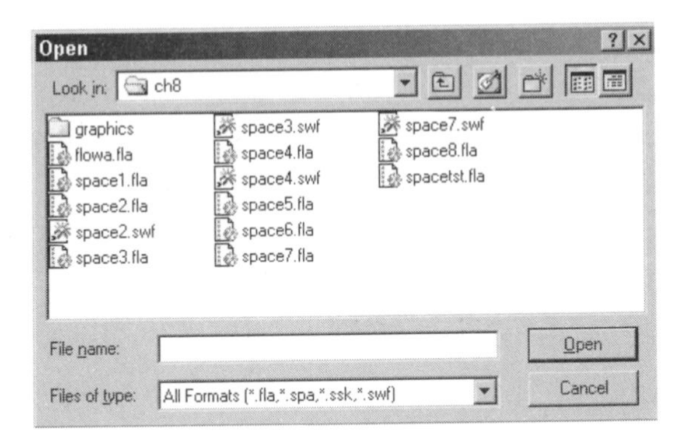

3. Select File ➢ Close to close the active movie. If it has not been saved, you will be prompted to save it.

4. Select File ➢ Save to save the active file, and select File ➢ Save As if you would like to change the filename or the location of the movie as you save it. If you have not yet saved the file you are working on, you will see the Save As dialog box. Save and Save As will both save the file.

Tip

When you choose Save, you should identify the folder in which you intend to look for the file the next time you want to work on it. That way, you will be able to retrieve it easily.

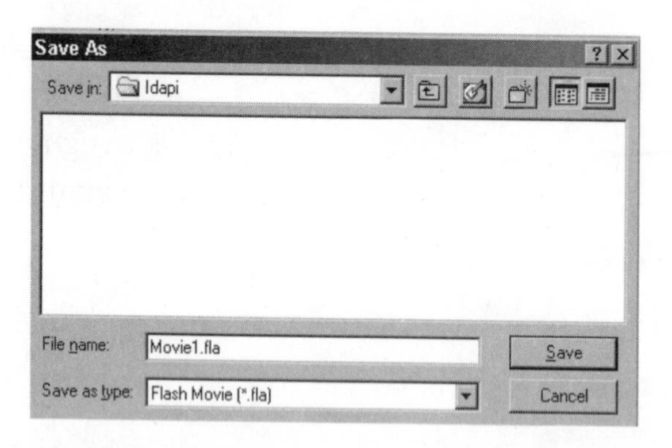

Opening Libraries

You can use the common libraries shipped with Flash to add symbols to your movies. You also can create your own permanent libraries to be used with future movies. When you use File ➢ Open as Library, you are opening only the library portion of a movie file:

1. Select File ➢ Open as Library. Use this command when you're working on a new movie and you want to access the symbols saved with a previous project. This will open the library of the previous movie, so that you can use it with the current movie.

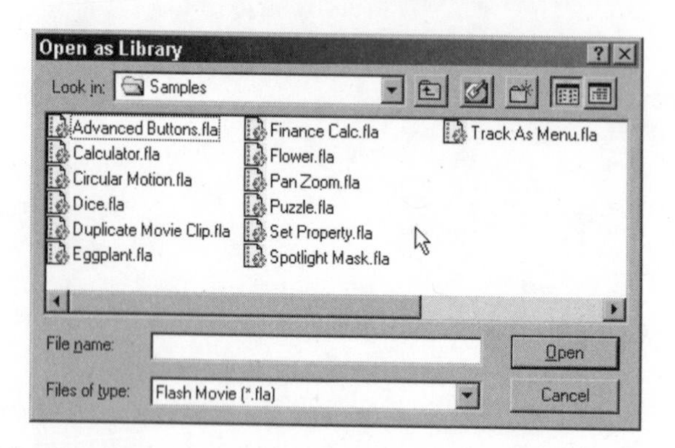

2. Select File ➢ Open as Shared Library to open a movie file and share its Library symbols across projects and among groups working on a single project.

Page Setup and Printing

The Page Setup command on the File menu is related to setting up the printed page. You also can change printer settings from the Printer button in the Page Setup dialog box. To become familiar with the page and printing setup options, follow these steps:

1. Select File ➢ Page Setup to view the options for margins, paper size and source, and layout. The Printer button (in the lower-right portion of the window) accesses the Print dialog box, which you can use to define how a page is printed.

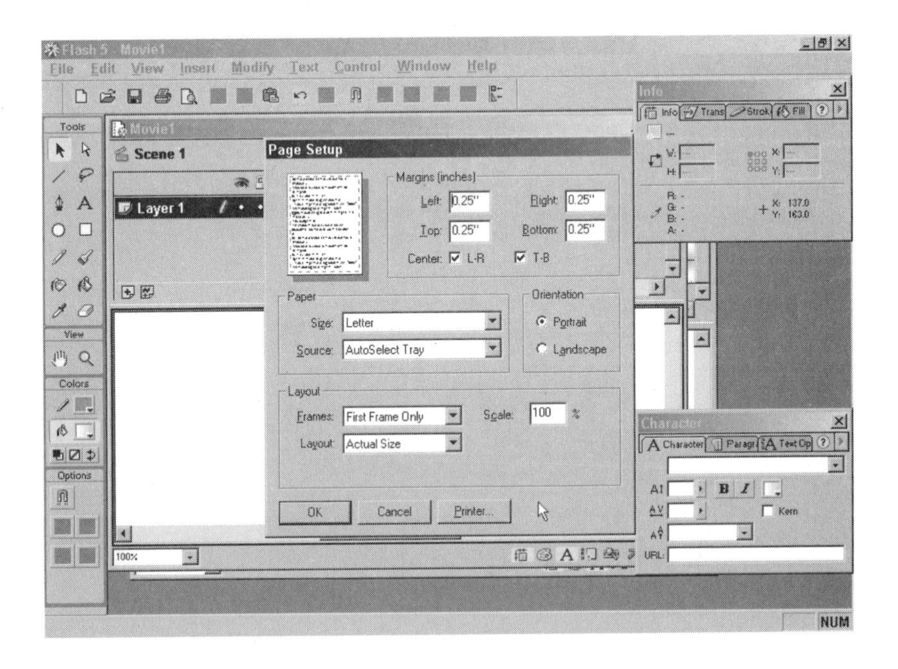

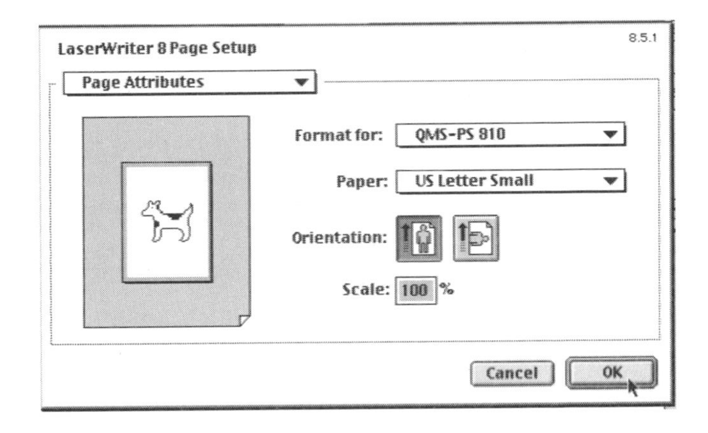

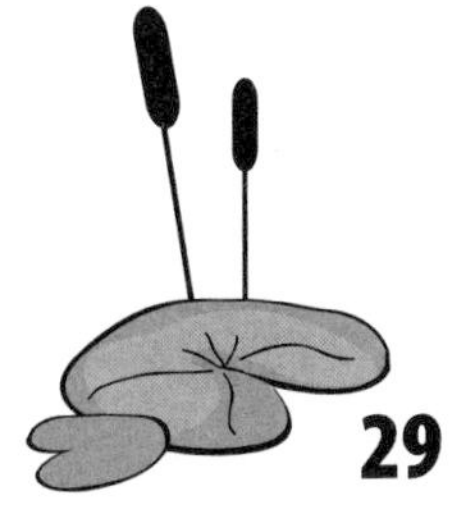

2. Select File ➢ Print to view the options for printing. You can designate the number of copies and the range of pages to print, you can print to a file, and you can click the Properties button to access the property sheet for your default or selected printer.

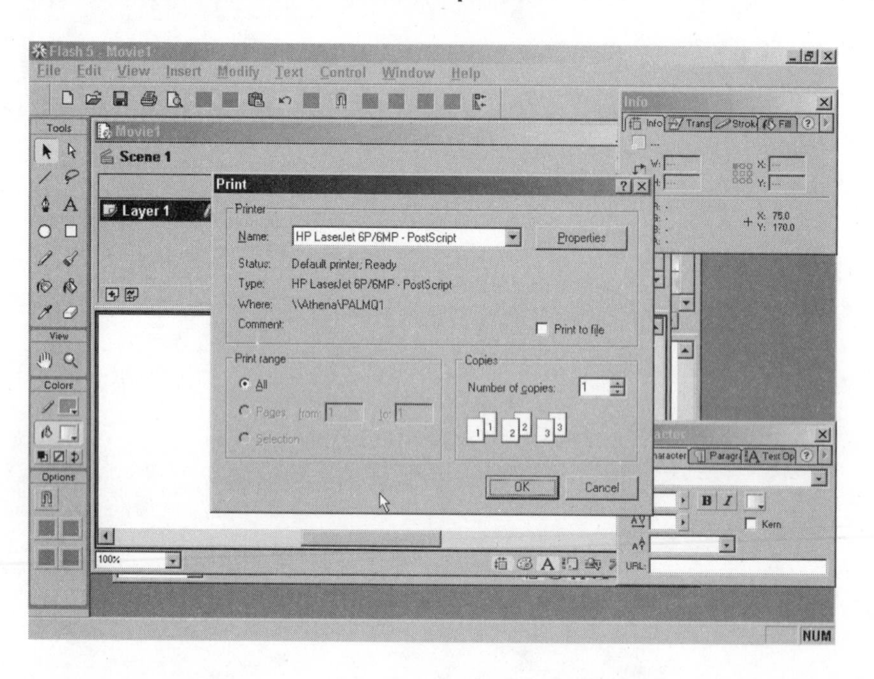

8.5.1
Printer: QMS-PS 810
Destination: ✓ Printer
File
General
Copies: 1 Collated
Pages: All
From: To:
Paper Source: All pages from: Cassette
First page from: Cassette
Remaining from: Cassette
Save Settings
Cancel Print

Send
Forwards the movie to an e-mail address.

E-Mailing Files

Select File ➢ **Send** to attach your movie to an e-mail message. The Send option in Windows is very handy if you want to send the movie as an attachment via e-mail. It launches your e-mail program with the current movie automatically

attached. The attached file is the FLA file, not the compiled SWF file. Thus, your recipients must have the Flash application installed on their systems to play the movie.

Note

The File ➢ Send option is not available on the Mac.

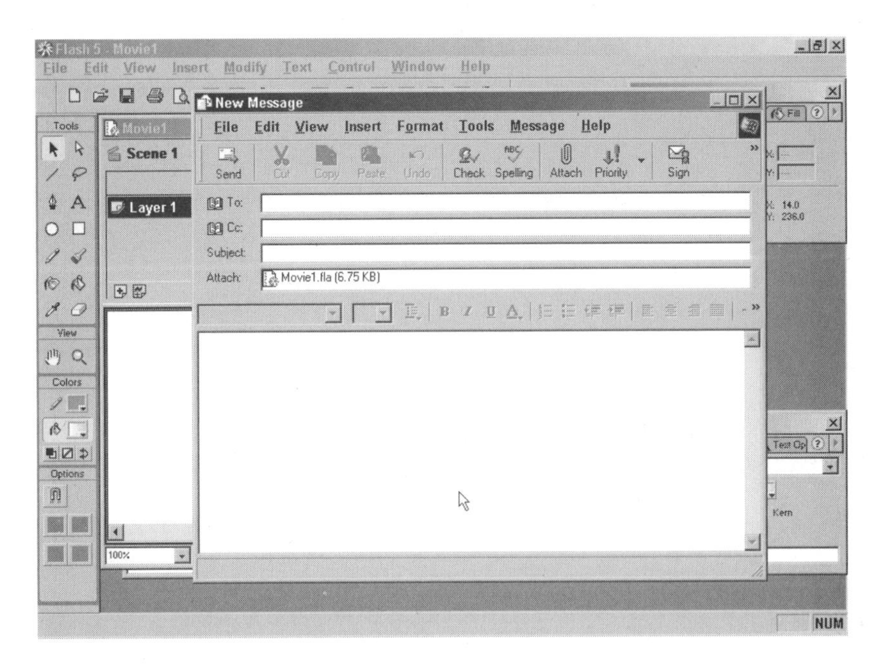

Using Editing Menu Commands

The Edit menu commands include most of the options available on the Toolbar for Windows users. The most common Edit commands allow you to undo, redo, cut, copy, and paste. You can also set your Flash preferences via the Edit menu.

Undoing and Redoing your Work

When you make a mistake, you can use Edit ➢ **Undo**. Redo simply re-creates the action that took place prior to the last undo:

1. Select Edit to view the Edit menu options.

Undo
Undoes the most recent change.

Tip

You must have work in progress on the Stage that acknowledges menu features in order to see the bolded format of these options. You cannot use the options when they are grayed out. For example, you can choose Edit Symbols only when there are symbols on your work area to edit.

Edit View Insert Modify Text Cor
Undo Ctrl+Z
Redo Ctrl+Y
Cut Ctrl+X
Copy Ctrl+C
Paste Ctrl+V
Paste in Place Ctrl+Shift+V
Paste Special...
Clear Backspace
Duplicate Ctrl+D
Select All Ctrl+A
Deselect All Ctrl+Shift+A
Cut Frames Ctrl+Alt+X
Copy Frames Ctrl+Alt+C
Paste Frames Ctrl+Alt+V
Edit Symbols Ctrl+E
Edit Selected
Edit All
Preferences...
Keyboard Shortcuts...

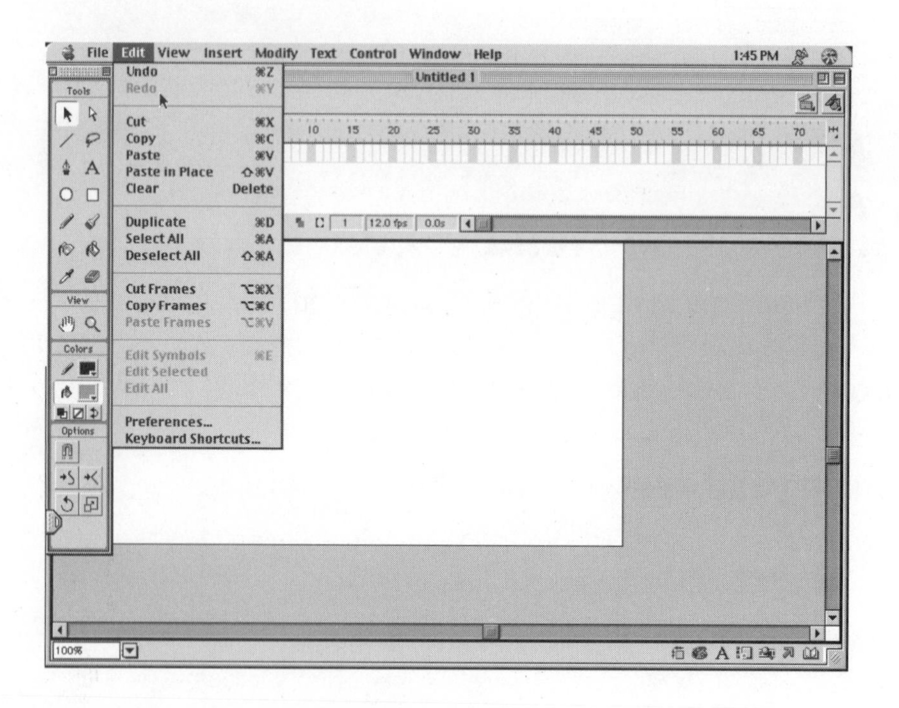

2. Use the Pencil tool to draw a line, then select Edit ➢ Undo. The line will disappear.

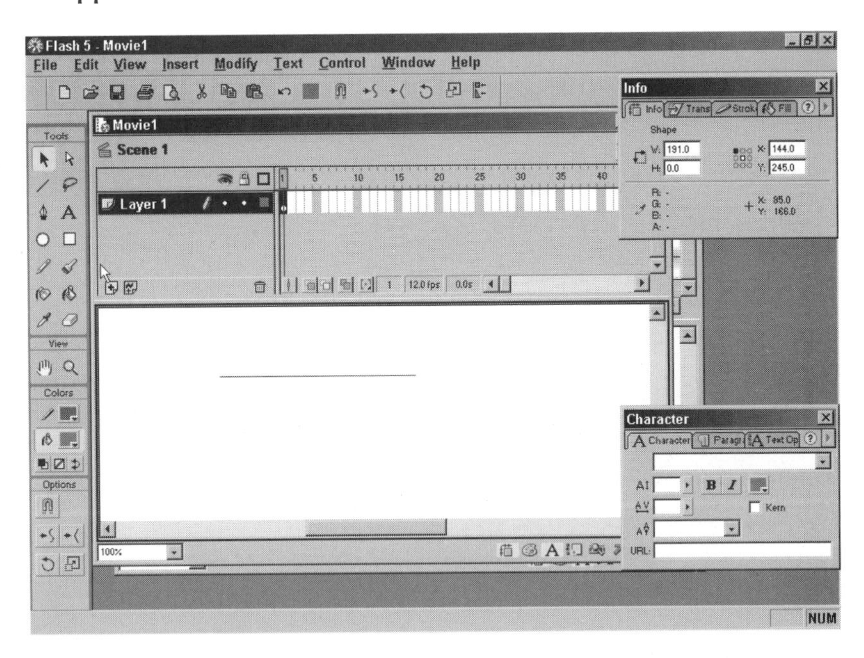

3. Click Redo on the Edit menu. Your line will be restored. Undo and Redo are also available on the Windows toolbar.

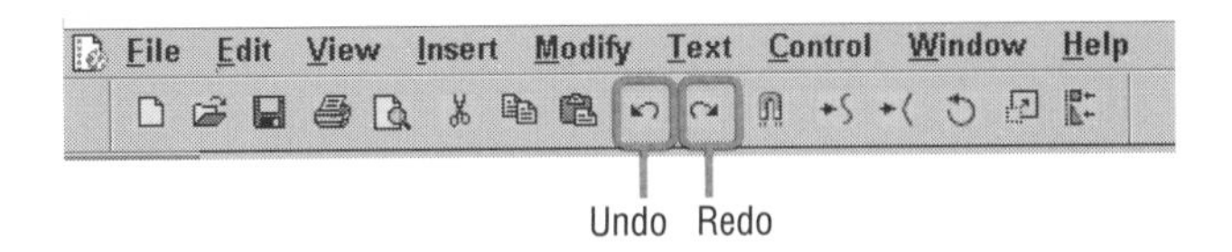

4. Select the line that is now restored by double-clicking or drawing a box around it with the Arrow tool.

Cutting, Copying, and Pasting Objects

These editing functions can be found in most types of word processing and graphics programs:

1. With the line selected, select Edit ➢ Cut. The line will disappear. Select Edit ➢ Undo again to restore the line.

Note

Many of the Edit menu options are available on the Standard toolbar in Windows.

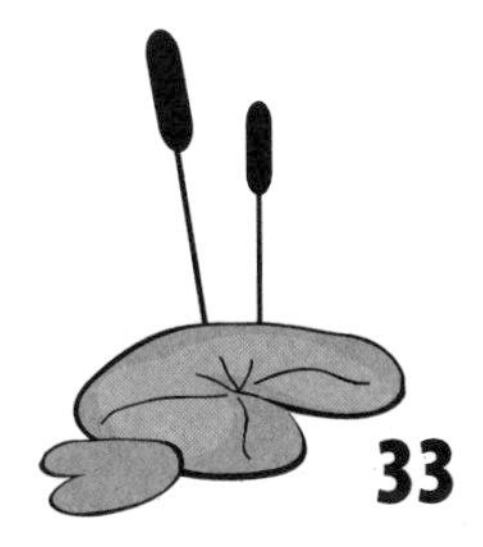

2. Select Edit ➢ Copy to copy the line to the Clipboard.

Note

The Paste option will not appear bolded on the menu until you have copied an object to the Clipboard.

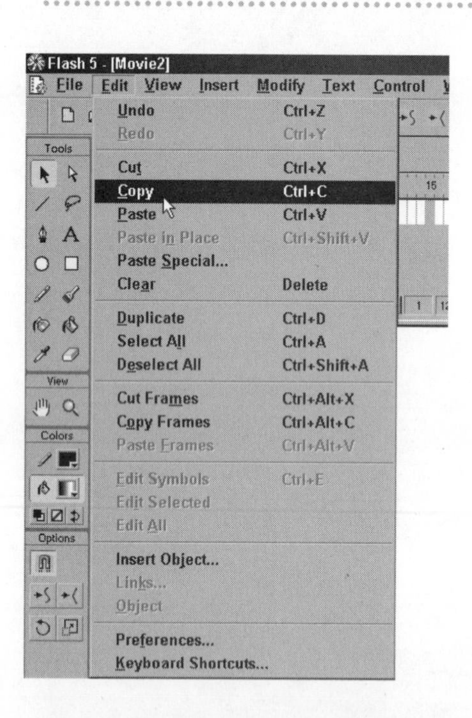

3. Select Paste to paste another copy onto the Stage.

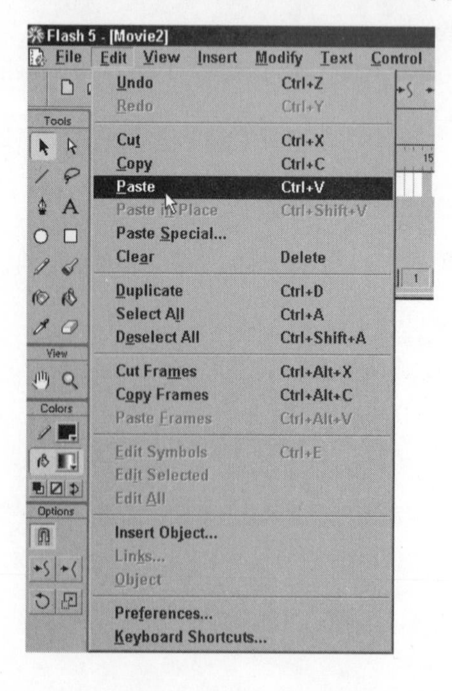

4. Select Edit ➢ Paste in Place to place another copy directly on the original line.

5. Select Edit ➢ Clear to delete your selected line. Remember to restore it by choosing Edit ➢ Undo.

Note

Paste in Place pastes the object at the same coordinates as the original.

Duplicating Objects

Duplicating is similar to copying, except that the duplicated object is not copied to the Clipboard:

Select Edit ➢ Duplicate to create a second copy of your selected line. Notice that the second line is a different color, indicating that it's selected (when you click outside the line to deselect it, it returns to its original color). This feature makes it easy to tell the original line from the duplicates.

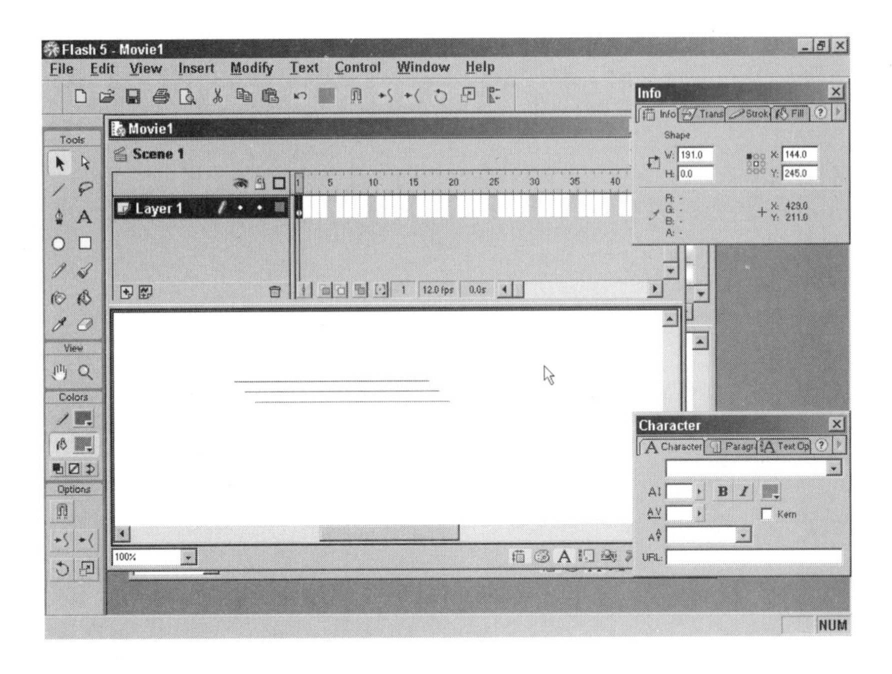

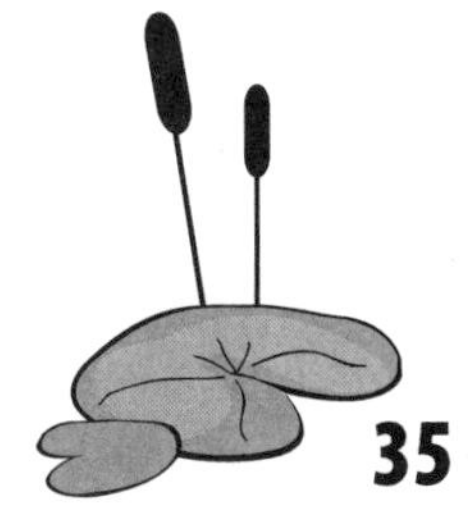

Selecting Objects

You can select all of the objects on the Stage by choosing Edit ➢ Select All. If you created a number of objects, such as two ovals and three rectangles, you could use Edit ➢ Select All to select them all and then choose Modify ➢ Group to group them. This is much faster than holding down the Shift key and clicking each object in turn until all are selected.

Use Edit ➢ Select All to select your lines. Then use Edit ➢ Deselect All to deselect them.

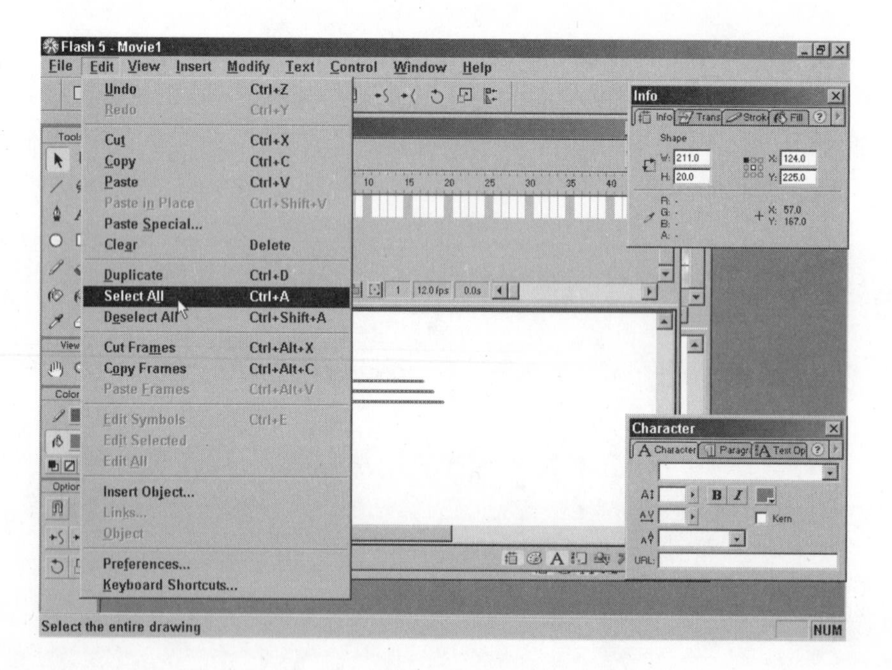

Pasting Objects

You can paste objects that are on the Clipboard. When you select Edit ➢ Cut to delete an item or Edit ➢ Copy to copy an item, it is saved to the Clipboard so that it can then be pasted into any Windows or Mac application, including the active application:

1. Launch an application such as a word processor or draw program that provides clip art objects. Insert an object on the page and select Copy to copy it to the Clipboard.

2. Return to Flash and Select Edit ➢ Paste Special (this option is not available on the Mac). You can paste from another application or from artwork or movies you created in Flash. Paste Special copies the contents of the Clipboard into the current movie.

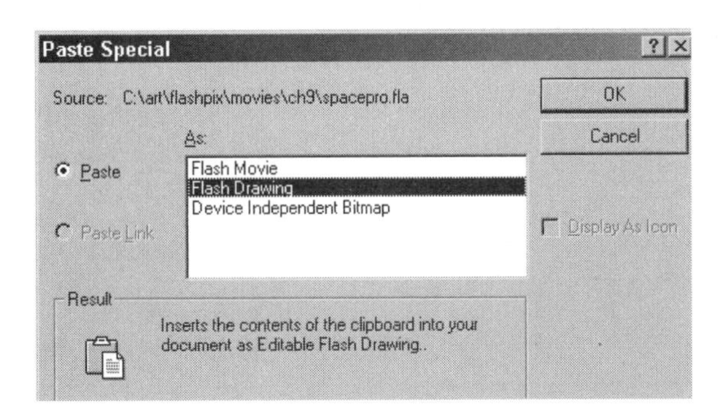

Managing Symbols from the Menu

As you learned in Chapter 1, you can convert existing objects to symbols or create new ones. You can access menu options from the context menus by right-clicking in Windows or using Ctrl+click on the Mac.

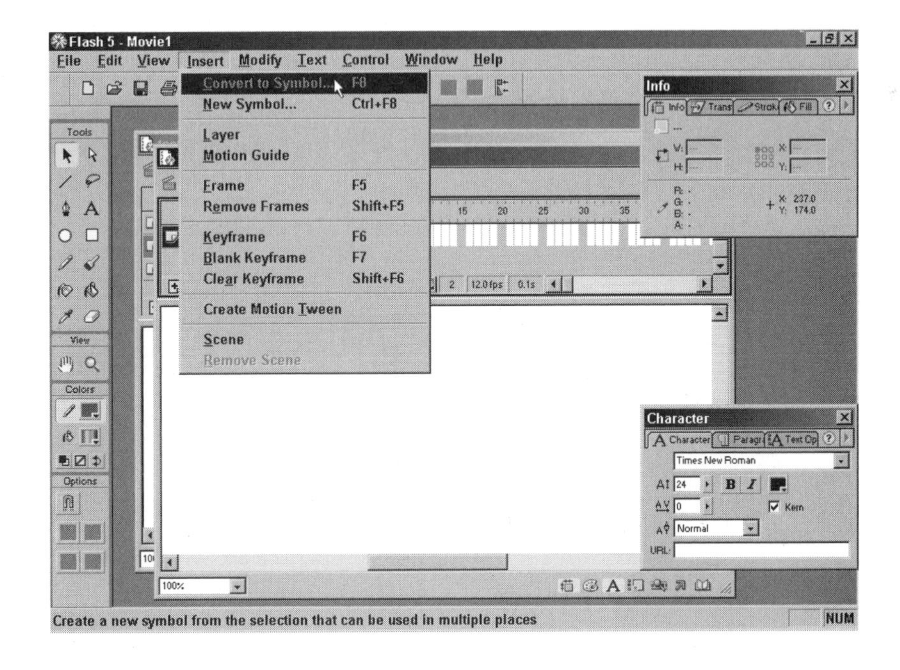

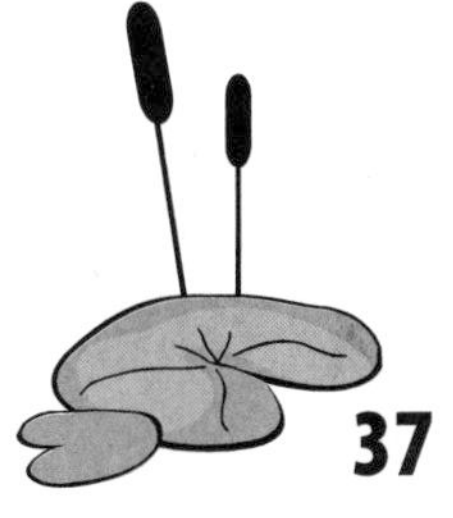

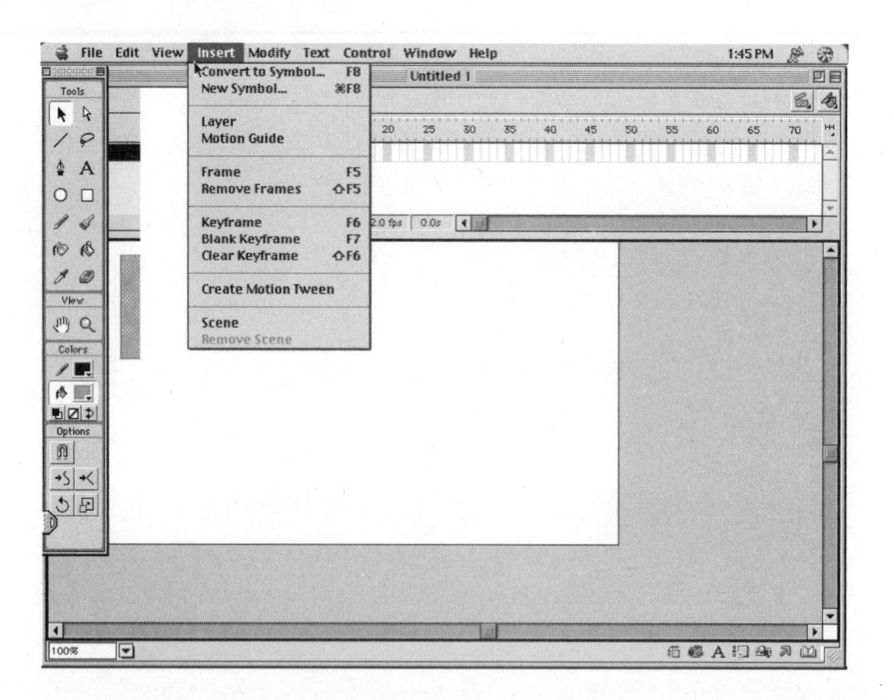

To work with symbols, follow these steps:

1. Select the artwork, then select Insert ➢ Convert to Symbol to transform the artwork into a reusable object. You can create instances of the symbol and use the different instances in different frames along the timeline.
2. Click Insert ➢ New Symbol. The Symbol Properties dialog box appears. Name the symbol "Button 1" and select the Button radio button in the Behavior section.

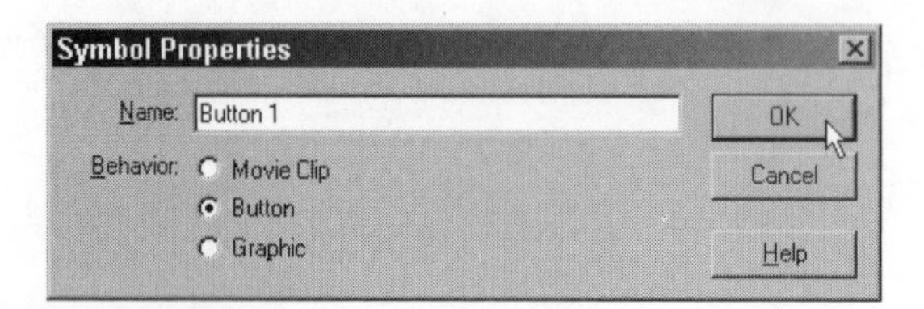

3. Create an object to take on the identity of the symbol you have named.
4. Select the Oval tool and draw an oval. Open the Library. Notice that the oval appears in the Library window above the name of the Button 1 symbol.

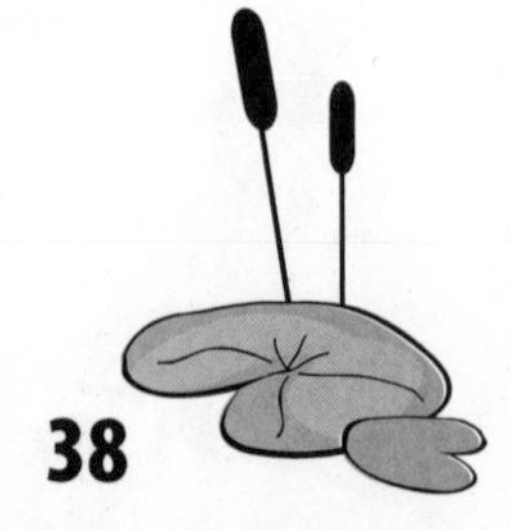

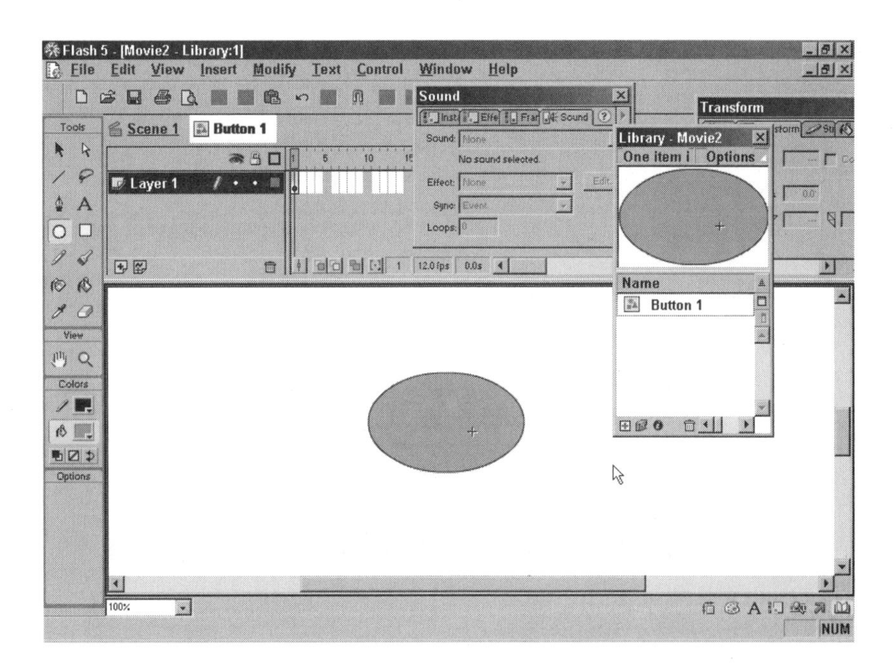

5. Now Select Insert ➢ New Symbol again. Name it "Symbol 2" and select the Graphic radio button.

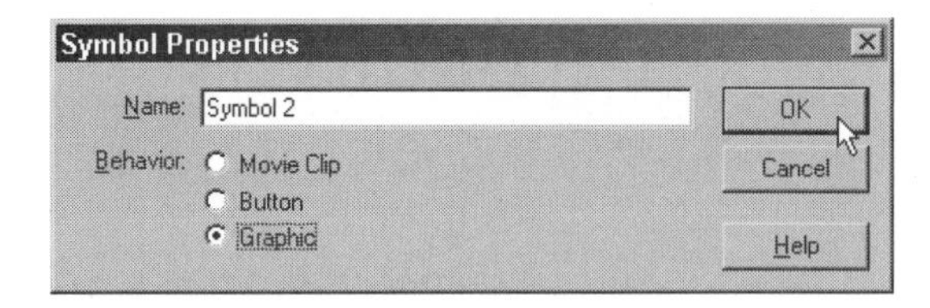

6. Once you click OK in the Symbol Properties dialog box, the name of the new symbol will appear in the Name pane of the Library window, under the name of the first symbol.

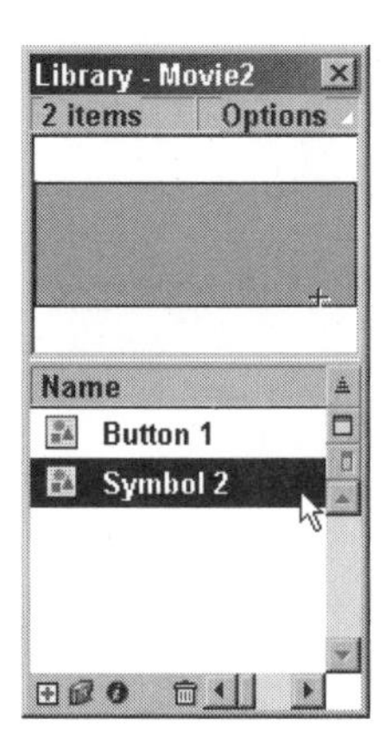

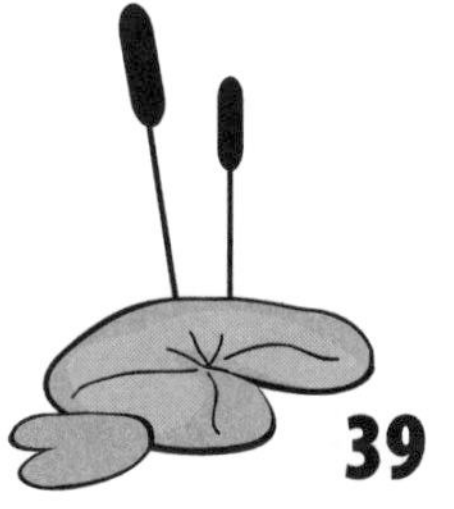

7. With the symbol in the Name pane of the Library window selected, select the Rectangle tool and draw a rectangle on the center of the Stage. Now the rectangle appears in the Items pane of the Library window.

Inserting Other Items

Several of the remaining Insert menu options are available from the context menus:

- The Layer and Motion Guide options are also on the context menu via a right-click (Ctrl+click on the Mac) when a layer is selected.

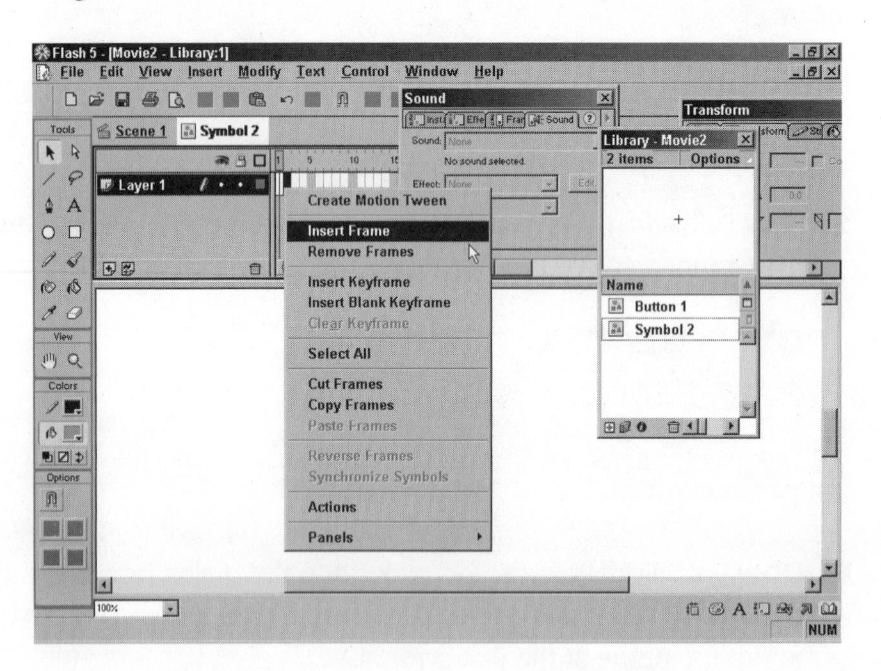

- The Insert menu items dealing with adding frames, removing frames, and adding and clearing keyframes and the Create Motion Tween option are also on the timeline context menu.
- The context menu options are available when you right-click (Ctrl+click on Mac) while a frame on the timeline is selected.

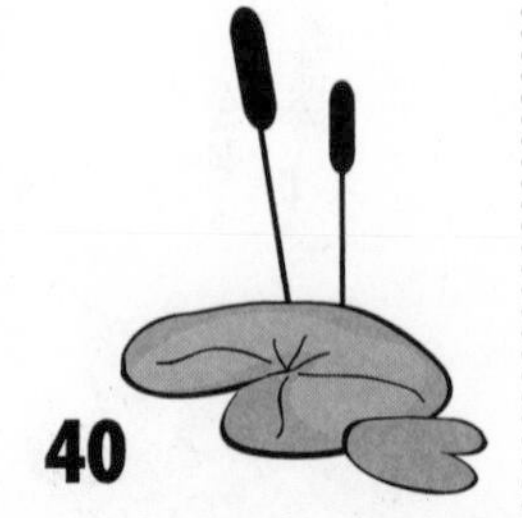

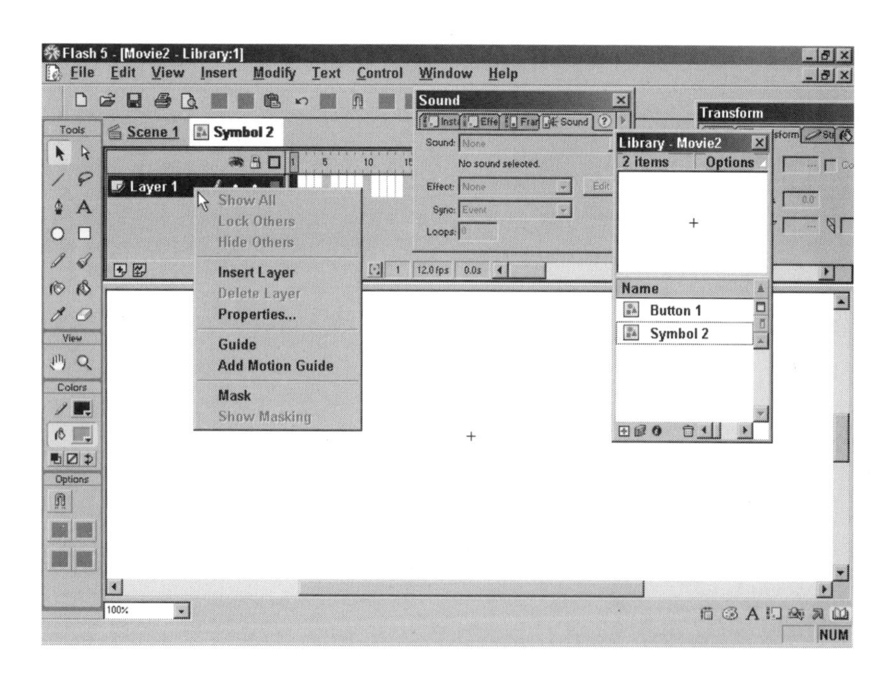

- The last two options on the Insert menu allow you to create a new movie scene and also to remove it.

Modifying Movie Properties

Many of the tools available in the Flash interface allow you to modify objects in your movie. With the Modify menu options, you can create, for example, color and sound effects.

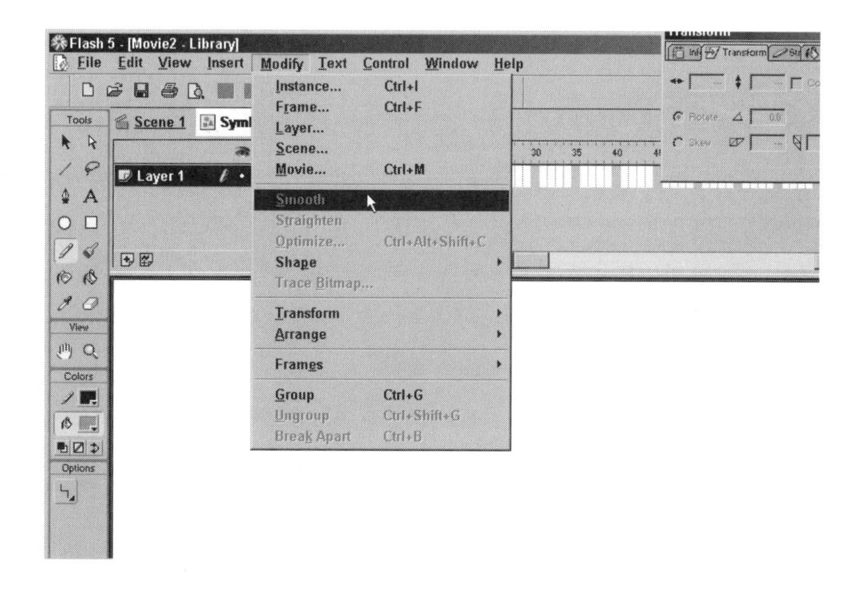

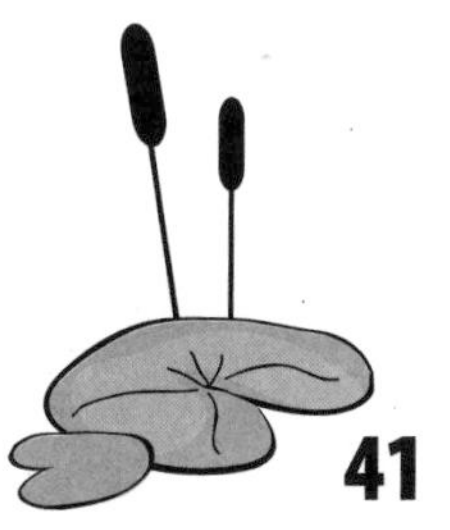

Here's a brief exercise to make you familiar with the Modify menu options:

1. Select Symbol 2 from the Library window after first selecting the Symbol 2 name. Select Modify ➢ Instance. Use the Instance Panel to set the behavior of the symbol you created in the last exercise.

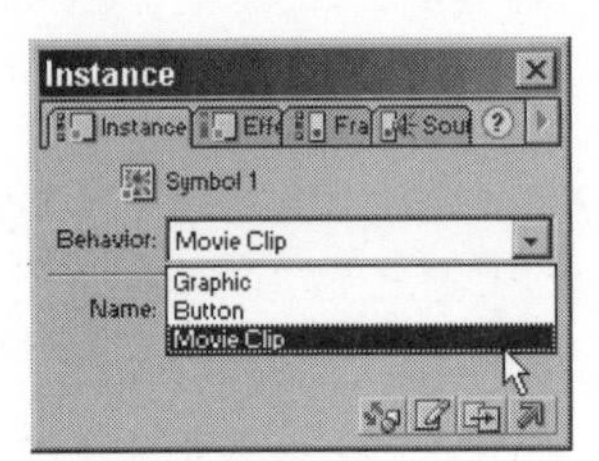

2. Select Modify ➢ Movie. View the properties of the movie that you can modify here. You can change the frame rate and Stage dimensions and match the size of the Stage to the printer page. You also can change the Stage background color and toggle the ruler units between pixels and other points of measurement, such as inches.

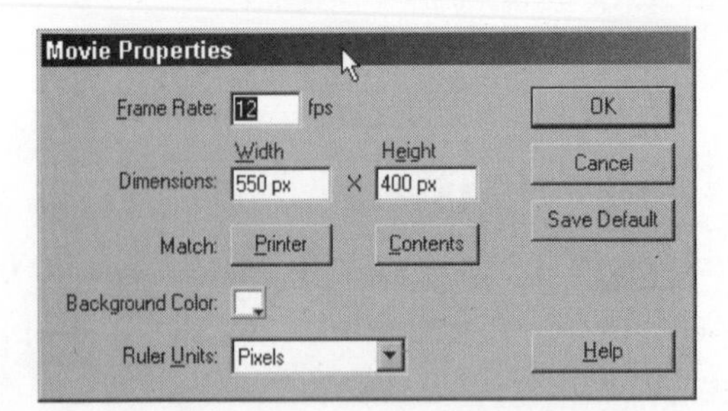

Accessing Tool Options from the Menu

Some Tool options are available from the Toolbox as well as from the menus. For example, you can use the tool modifiers in the Options box below the Toolbox, but you also can make modifications by selecting menu options.

Tool Modify Options on the Menu

Some tool modifiers are found in several places. For example, the Smooth, Straighten, and Rotate tool modifiers are found in the Options box below the

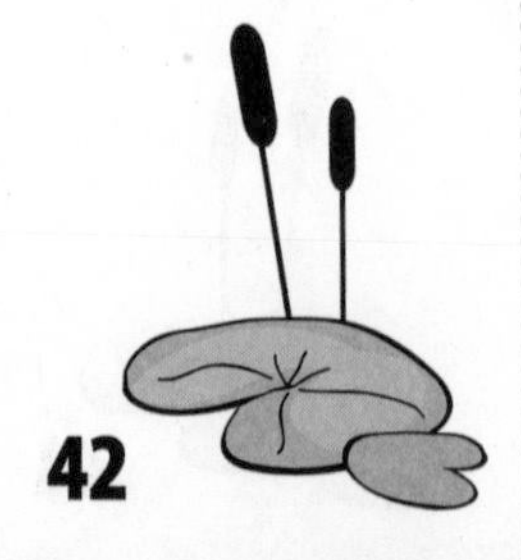

Toolbox, on the Windows toolbar, and on the Modify menu. However, some of the options that affect tools (such as the Convert Lines to Fills, Expand Fill, and Soften Fill Edges) are available only from the Modify menu:

1. Select the Line tool, and then select black for the line color by clicking the Color button next to the Pencil tool in the Colors box under the Toolbox.
2. Draw a rough box. Select the Arrow tool, then select the box you just drew. Select Modify ➢ Shape ➢ Convert Lines to Fills. Select the Fill Color button in the Colors box below the Toolbox and change the fill color to something other than black or white. The lines will change to your selected fill color.

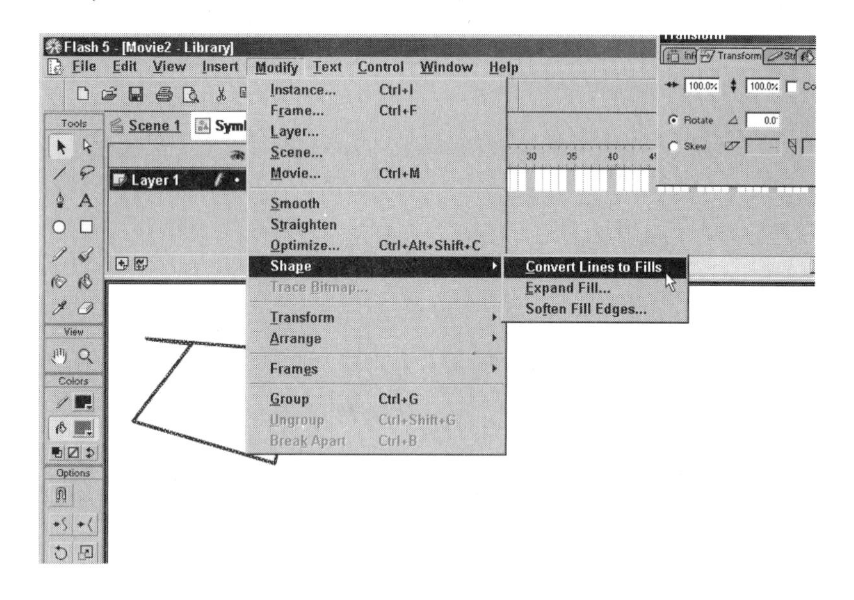

3. Select the lines again, choose Modify ➢ Shape ➢ Expand Fill.
4. Make sure the Distance parameter is set to 4 pixels (4 px) and check the Expand box. Click OK. The lines will become thicker.

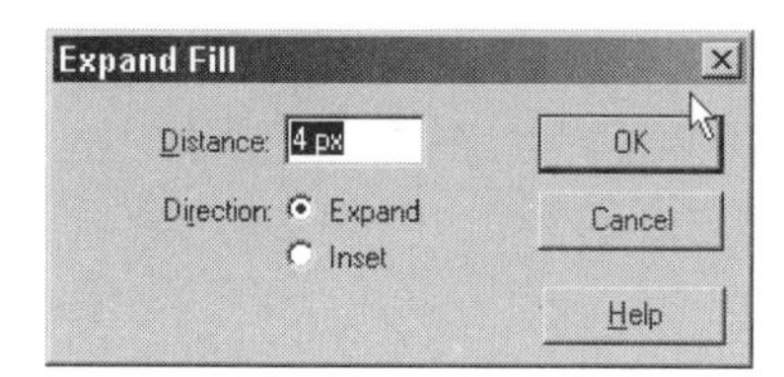

5. Select Modify ➢ Shape ➢ Soften Fill Edges. Now the edges become even thicker and rounded as well. You can enter a value for the distance (in pixels), the number of steps you want to take to complete the softening, and whether you want the fill to expand or to be inset. Softening the edges modifies the pixels to create a somewhat blurred effect.

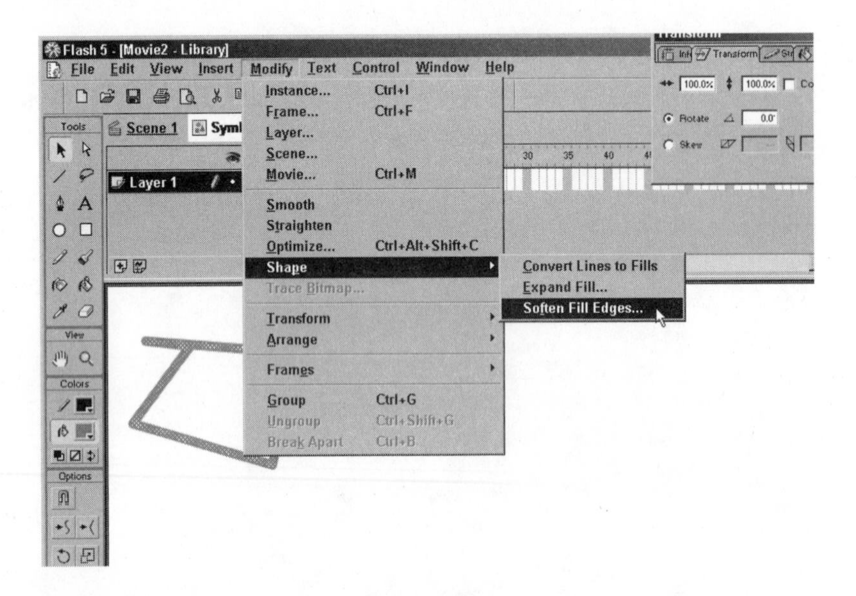

6. Select Modify ➢ Transform and then choose Rotate 90°CW (clockwise). The figure you drew will rotate.

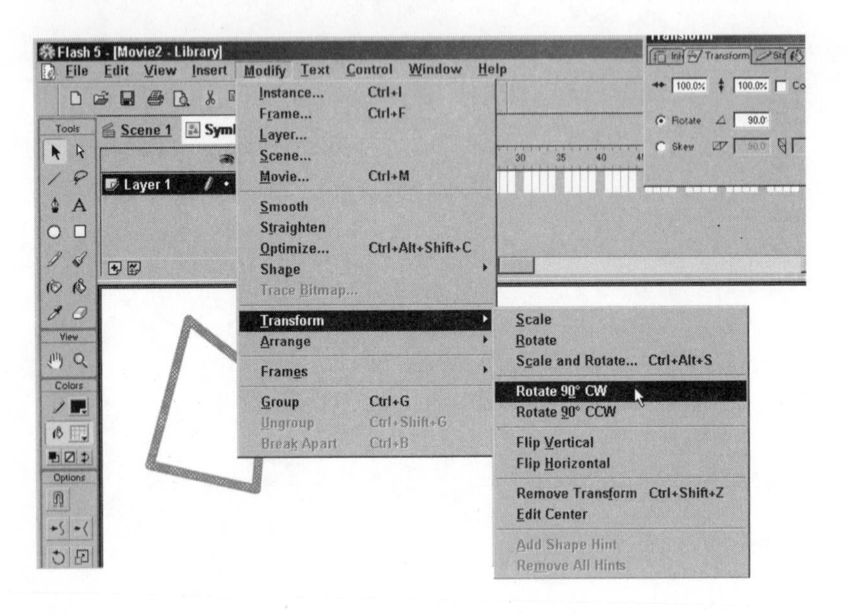

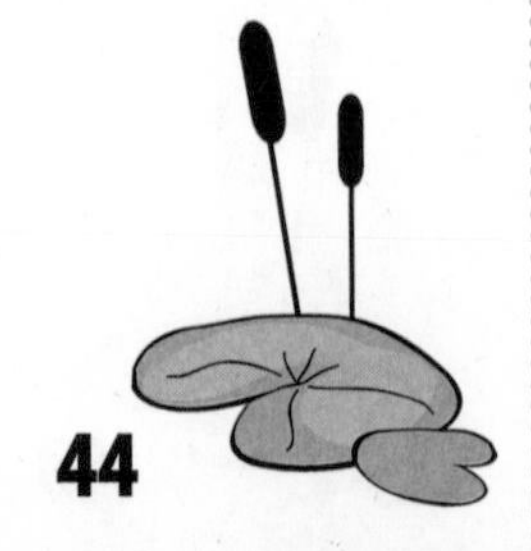

Controlling Your Movie

There are a number of tools available to you in the Control menu. You can choose Play, Rewind, Step Forward, and Step Backward to play back and test your movies.

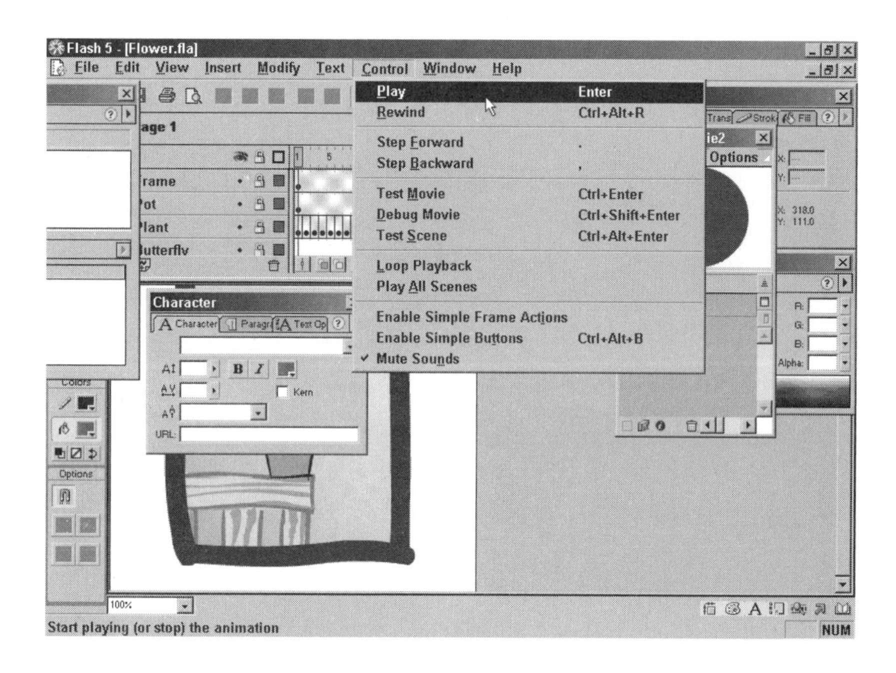

The Control ➢ Test Movie option plays the movie in a continuous loop, whereas the Play option plays it only once. To replay it, you must select Rewind, then Play. Alternatively, you can select Control ➢ Loop Playback, and then the movie will continually loop under the Play option.

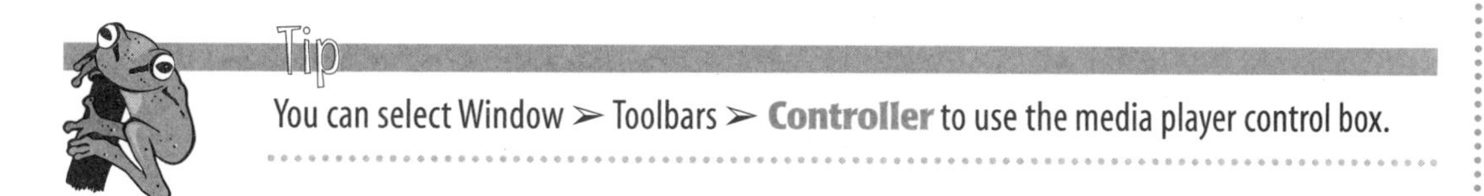

Tip

You can select Window ➢ Toolbars ➢ **Controller** to use the media player control box.

Controller
The Controller is a media controller with Play, Stop, Step Back, Rewind, Step Forward, and End controls.

Let's experiment with the options on the Control menu:

1. Select a movie by choosing one of the samples from the Help menu.
2. Choose Control ➢ Test Movie and view the movie.

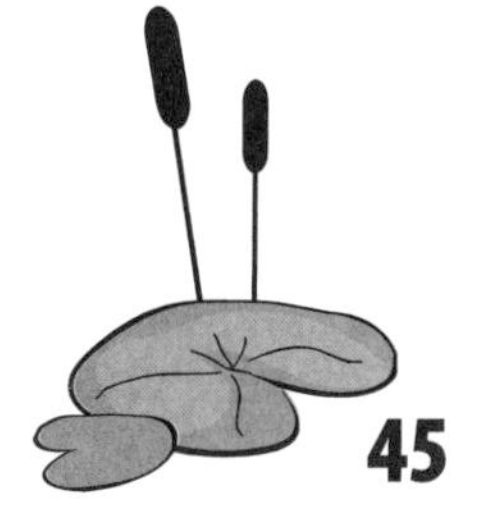

Note

When you select Control ➢ Play, only the current scene is played through all the frames in the timelines, whereas when you select Test Movie, all of the scenes are played and the movie will be compiled into the Flash Player movie `.swf` format. The compiled movie can be played on a machine without having the Flash application installed.

Customizing Flash

It is important for an application to allow users some modification of the working environment. Not everyone has the same skill level, physical capabilities, and needs. When you select Edit ➢ Preferences, you can define certain aspects of Flash that will let you customize your environment. I have made some suggestions here to get you started, but you should experiment with your Preferences settings to see what works best for you.

Managing the Interface

You can set up Flash to work like you do. Here are some basics to get you started:

1. Select Edit ➢ Preferences and click the General tab to view the options.

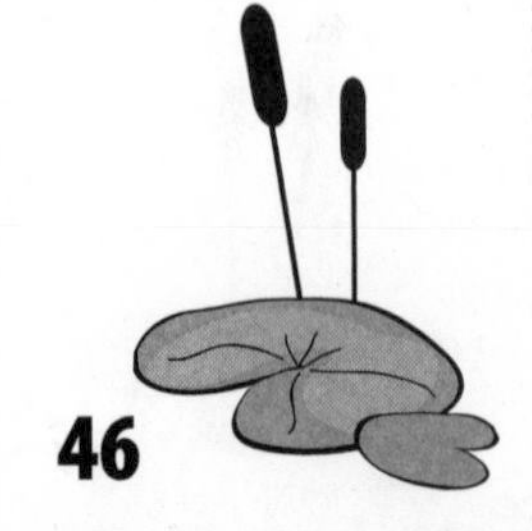

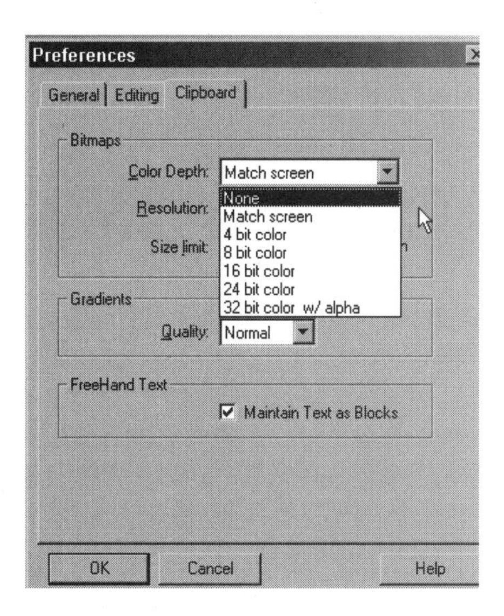

2. Change the **Undo Levels** setting to 50 or even lower by typing the number into the Undo Levels box.

Undo Levels
Determines how many consecutive actions can be undone.

Tip

The Undo Levels default setting is 100. Changing the setting to 50 allows you to undo 50 actions. That should be ample and will conserve system resources.

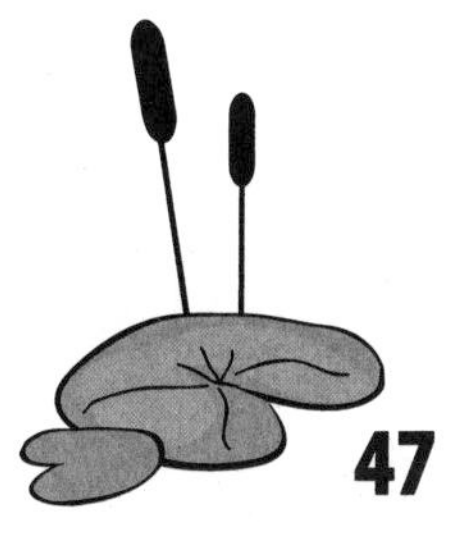

3. Check Shift Select to allow you to select several objects by holding down the Shift key while clicking the mouse button. If you deselect the check box, you will not be able to use Shift Select.
4. Check the Show Tooltips check box. It will toggle the tooltips display on and off.
5. Under Timeline Options, uncheck the Disable Timeline Docking box. When checked, this option will keep the timeline window from redocking after you have moved it to a floating position.
6. Uncheck the box beside Flash 4 Selection Style. This option will display the Flash interface as it looks in a previous version.
7. Click the Color button under Highlight color to change the default color or select the radio button to use the layer color.
8. Select Normal Mode from the Mode drop-down menu in the Actions Panel section. The Actions Panel can be accessed from the Window menu. You use the Actions Panel to assign actions to objects.

Controlling the Tools

You can set your preferences to control the precision you have when drawing lines, curves, and shapes and to control mouse-click accuracy. Select Edit ➢ Preferences and click the Editing tab to view the options.

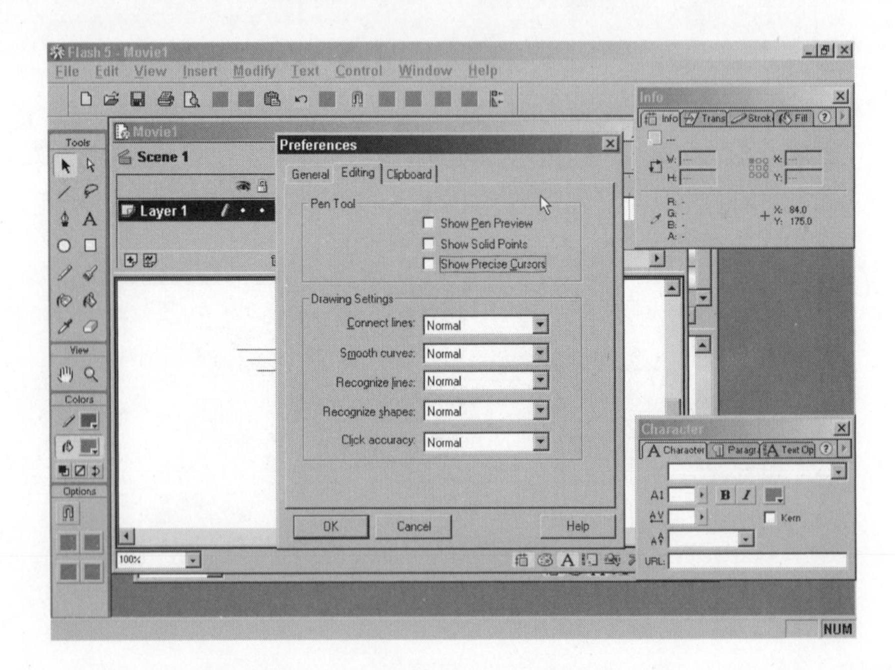

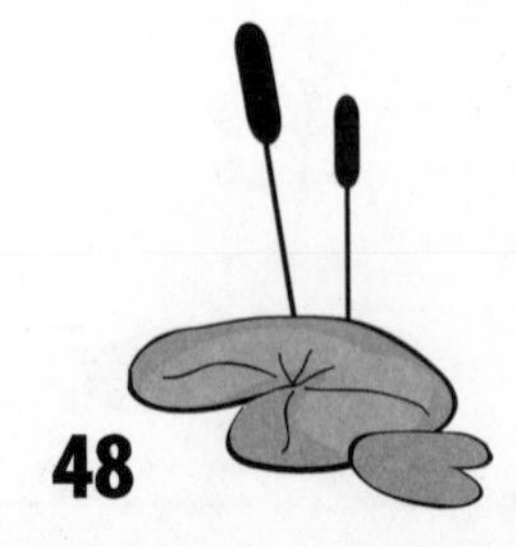

Setting Pen Tool Preferences

When you select the Pen Preview option, you can see where the line will be drawn before you click to complete it:

1. Select the Show Pen Preview option and click OK.
2. Select the Pen tool, click the mouse button and move the cursor to a new location, then click again. Continue moving the pen and clicking to draw a rectangle or polygon.

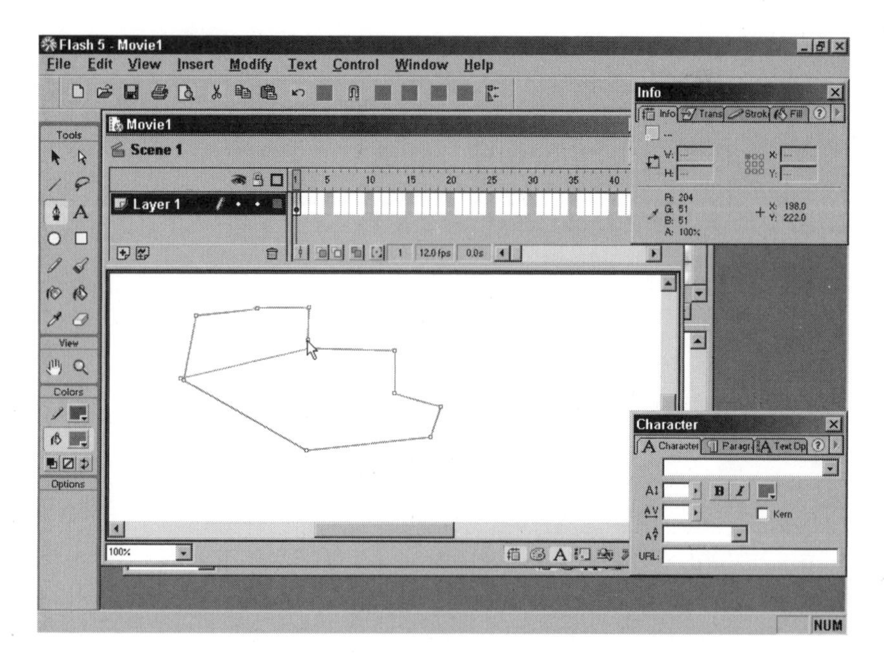

3. Open the Preferences window again and select the Editing tab. Uncheck the Show Pen Preview box.
4. Use the Pen tool to draw again. Because you unchecked the Show Pen Preview box, you will not see the line until you click to complete it (there will be no preview of the line).
5. View the points between each line. They are hollow by default.
6. Select the Editing tab in the Preferences window once again (Edit ➢ Preferences). Check the Show Solid Points box. Click OK and return to the Stage to draw some more lines. Notice that the points are now solid.

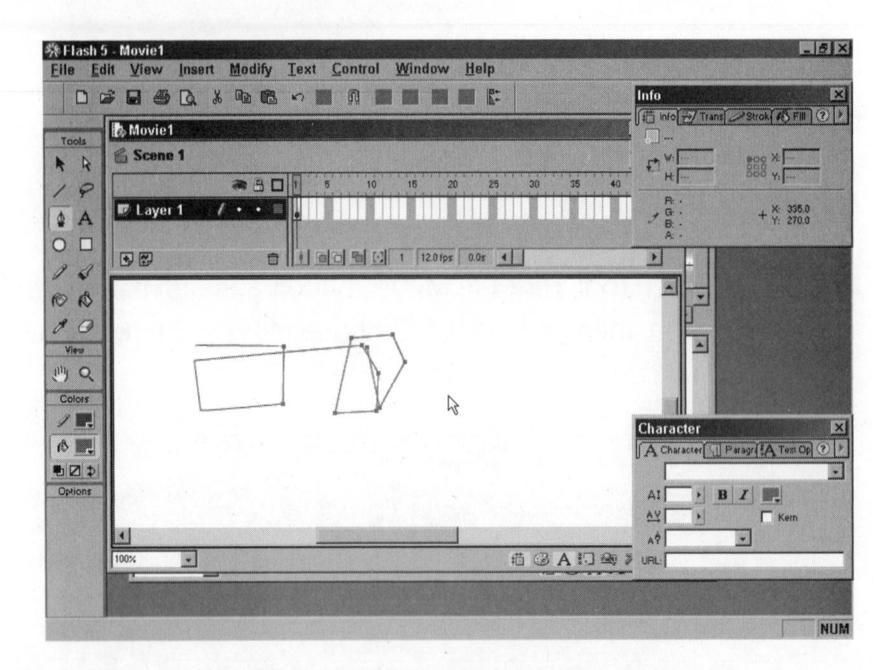

7. Check the Show Precise Cursors box to change the Pen into a crosshair shape to provide greater accuracy with the tool.

Setting Drawing Preferences

The Editing tab provides drawing settings that can be used if you want greater control when you're drawing lines and shapes. And it is on the Editing tab that you can set the accuracy of the mouse-click.

Connect Lines
Determines how close together lines must be drawn before Flash will connect them.

Connecting Lines

The **Connect Lines** setting controls how far apart lines can be drawn and still be considered connected:

1. Click the arrow next to the Connect Lines drop-down menu.
2. View the options for connecting lines. Leave this setting at Normal. Must Be Close means that lines must be close to one another to be considered connected. Can Be Distant means that lines that are distant from one another can be considered connected. If you have trouble drawing

connected lines, for example, you might choose the Can Be Distant option to make sure lines you want to connect do in fact connect.

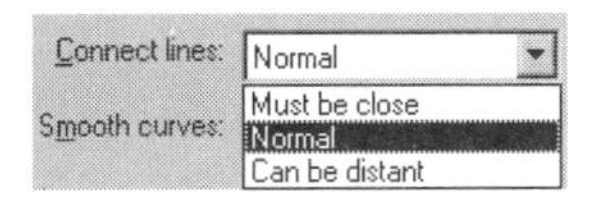

Smoothing Curves

The **Smooth Curves** setting controls the degree of smoothness in curves, from no control (off) to smooth:

1. Click the arrow next to the Smooth Curves drop-down menu.
2. View the options for smoothing curves in your drawing. Retain the Normal setting.

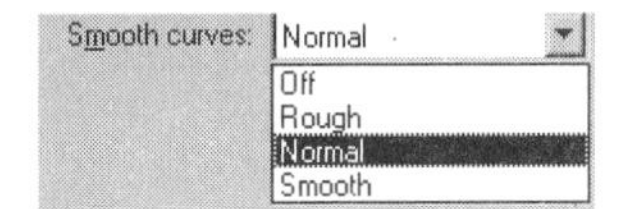

Smooth Curves
Determines how smooth curves will be when you draw them.

Recognizing Lines

The **Recognize Lines** setting determines the degree of straightness required in a line segment for Flash to recognize it and make it perfectly straight (if your lines are often very crooked, you should select the Tolerant option):

1. Click the arrow next to the Recognize Lines drop-down menu.
2. View the setting options. The setting should remain at Normal.

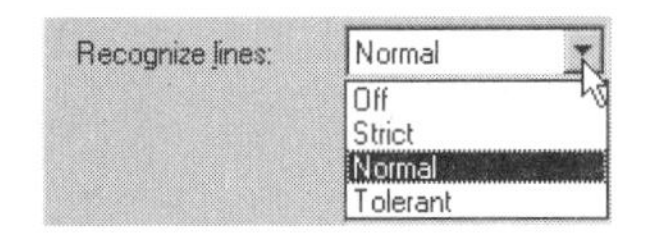

Recognize Lines
Determines how straight a line must be for Flash to see it as a line.

Recognizing Shapes

The **Recognize Shapes** setting determines how closely your shapes (circles, ovals, rectangles, squares, and arcs) must be drawn for Flash to see them as geometric shapes and correct them. Flash will convert any shape you draw with the Pencil provided it approximates a geometrical shape. Turning off the Recognize

Recognize Shapes
Determines how accurately shapes and arcs must be drawn in order for Flash to recognize them.

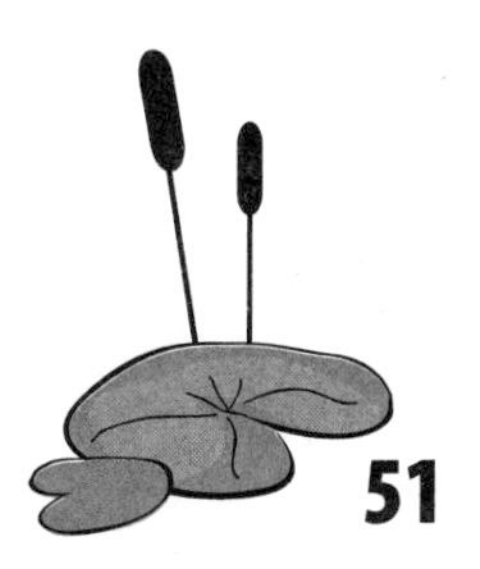

Shapes feature will result in crudely drawn shapes not being corrected to the nearest geometric shape:

1. Click the arrow next to the Recognize Shapes drop-down menu.

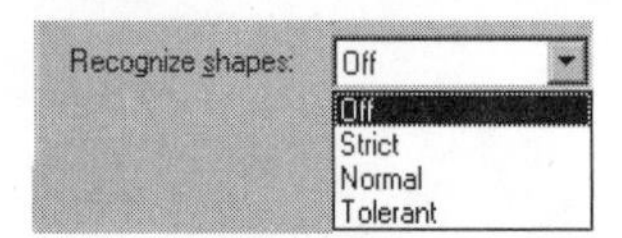

2. View the options. Turn this feature off by changing the setting to Off.
3. Select the Pencil tool from the Toolbox. On the Stage, draw a box. Do not try to draw a perfect square or rectangle. Just draw as if you were doodling. Note that the lines are straightened but that the box is not a square or rectangle.
4. Change the Recognize Shapes setting to Tolerant.

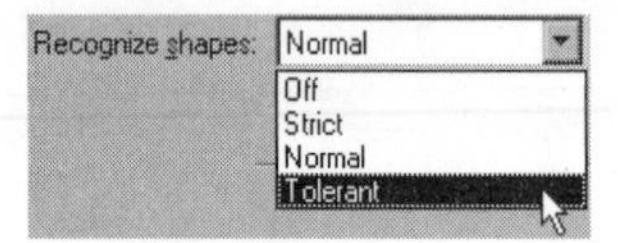

5. Draw another box similar in accuracy to the first. Does the box look much more like a rectangle than the first?

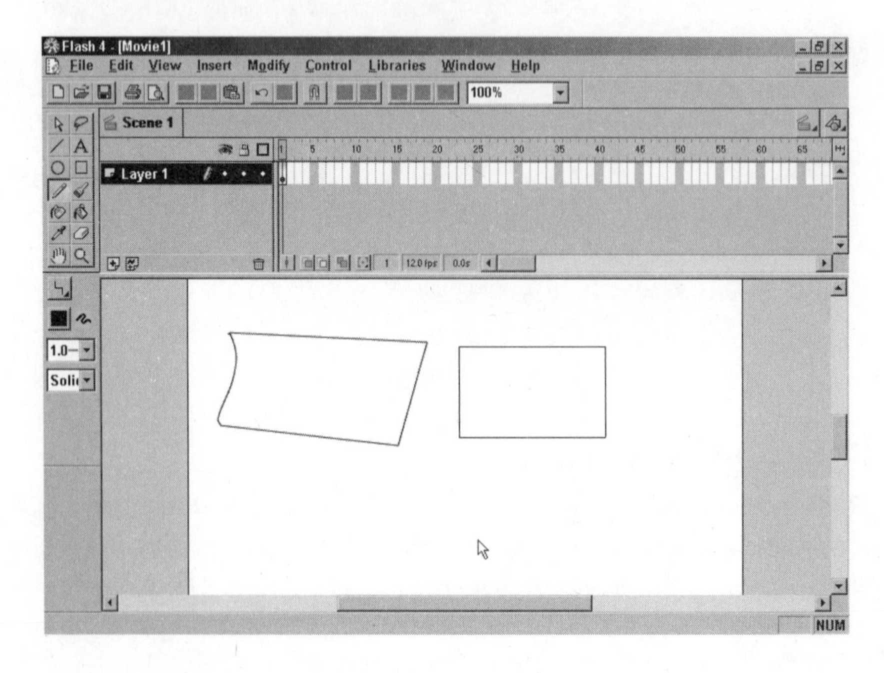

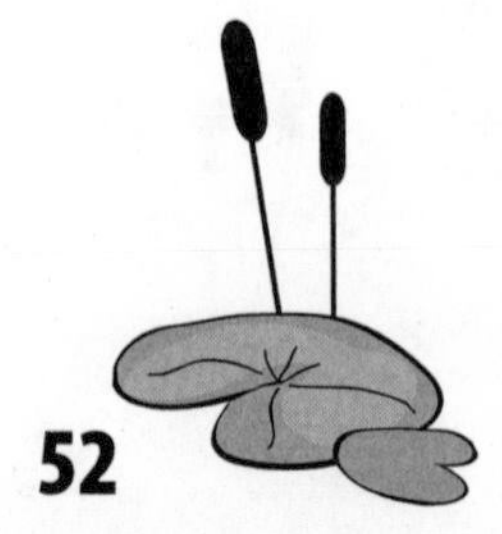

Controlling the Precision of the Mouse-Click

The Click Accuracy setting determines how close the cursor must be to an object for the mouse-click to select the object. With the Strict setting, the cursor needs to be right on the item to be selected. With the Tolerant setting, the cursor can be some distance away. Let's try it:

Click Accuracy
Determines how close the cursor needs to be to an object for the item to be selected.

1. Click the arrow next to the Click Accuracy drop-down menu.
2. View the options. Retain the Normal setting.

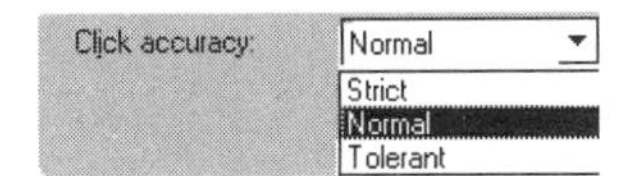

Dealing with Objects on the Clipboard

Color Depth, Resolution, Size Limit, and Smooth are among the options available on the Clipboard tab in the Preferences window.

resolution
The degree of detail that can be viewed in a graphic. Resolution is most often expressed in pixels per square inch.

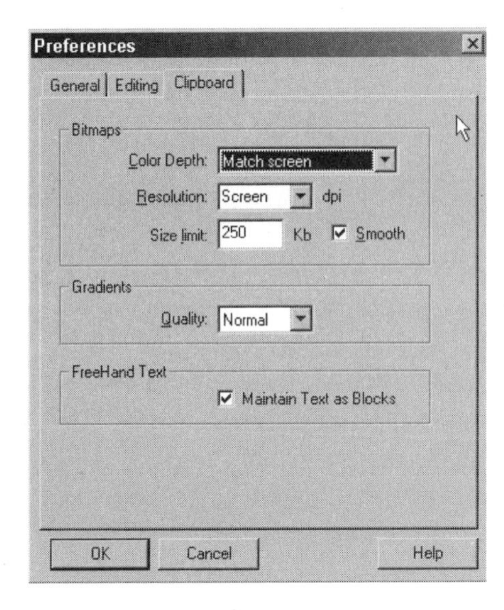

Note

When you copy objects to the Clipboard on the Mac, a PICT file is generated. The PICT settings can be used to determine the type of copy made. Mac users should select the Object option when copying. Using the Bitmaps options will result in poorer quality pastes. Using the Object option preserves the original vector graphic format.

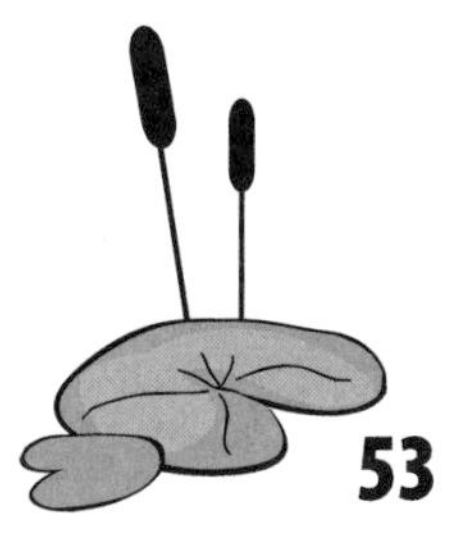

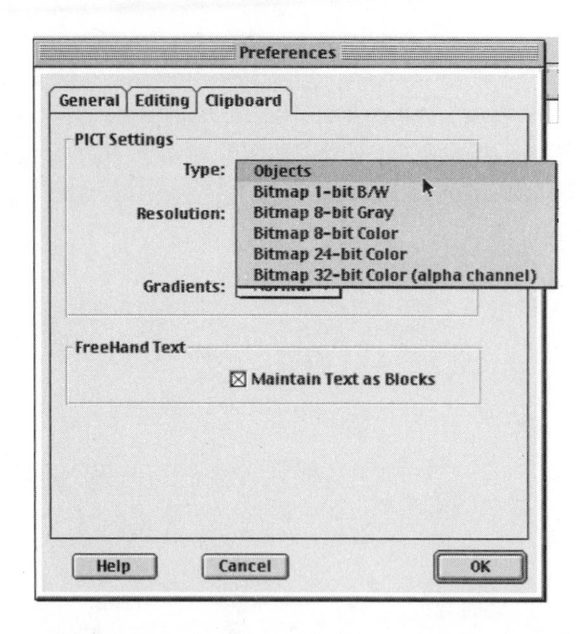

Image Preferences

You can control the quality of bitmaps you paste into other applications from Flash. For example, color depth, which controls the quality of bitmaps only, is one of the image preferences options (color depth is not an available option on the Mac). The first drop-down menu on the Clipboard tab allows you to select the color depth.

You can get similar effects on your computer system if you change the display settings to 16 color and then back to your normal settings to high (16-bit) or true (32-bit) color.

Note

You can control the quality of the color of the objects you copy to and from the Clipboard by setting them in your preferences just as you can change your Windows or Mac display from 256 colors to 16-bit or high color.

This quick exercise will demonstrate the differences between graphics copied from the Clipboard using different color depth settings:

1. Select the Oval tool in the Toolbox and draw an oval on the Stage.

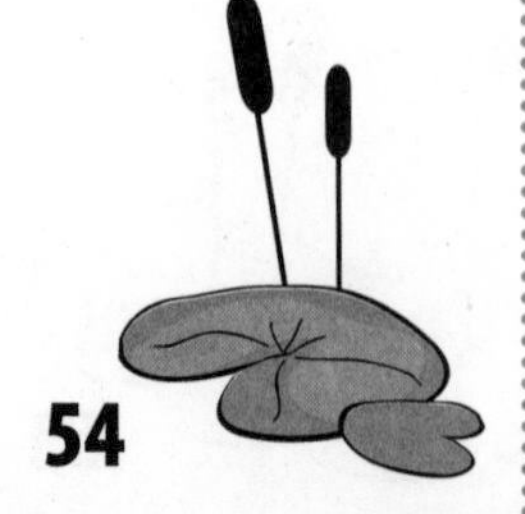

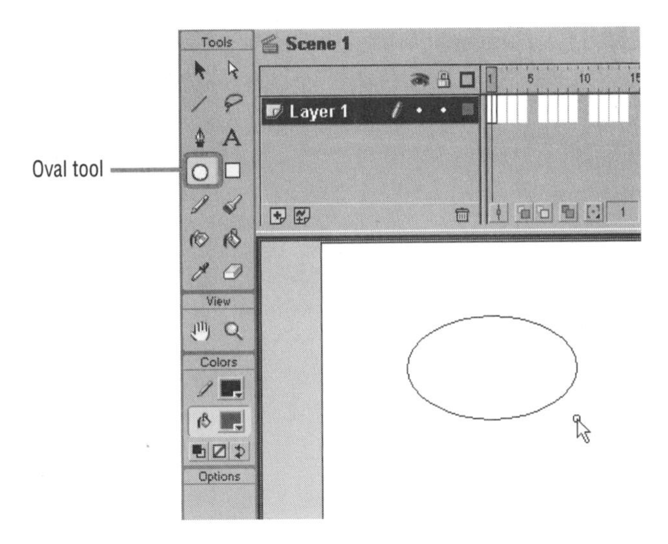

2. Select the Paint Bucket tool, then click the Color icon in the Tool modifier area. Choose a gradient fill. They are at the bottom of the Fill palette. With the Paint Bucket tool, click inside the oval.

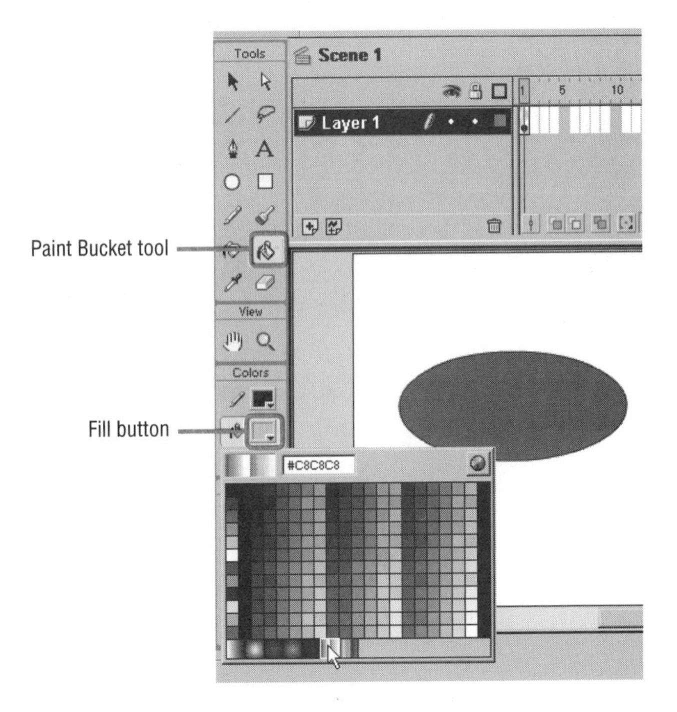

3. Select the Text tool from the Toolbox and change the font size to 24 points. Write a short message on the oval.

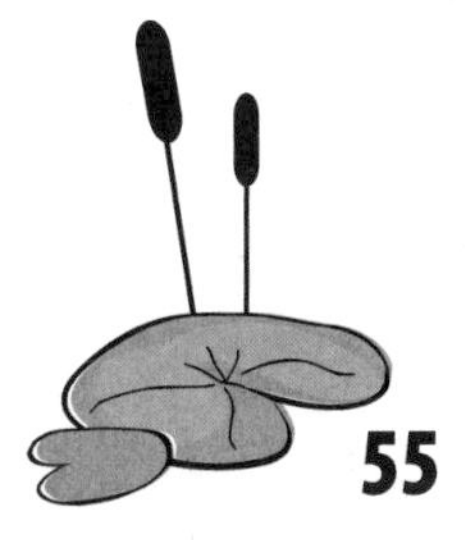

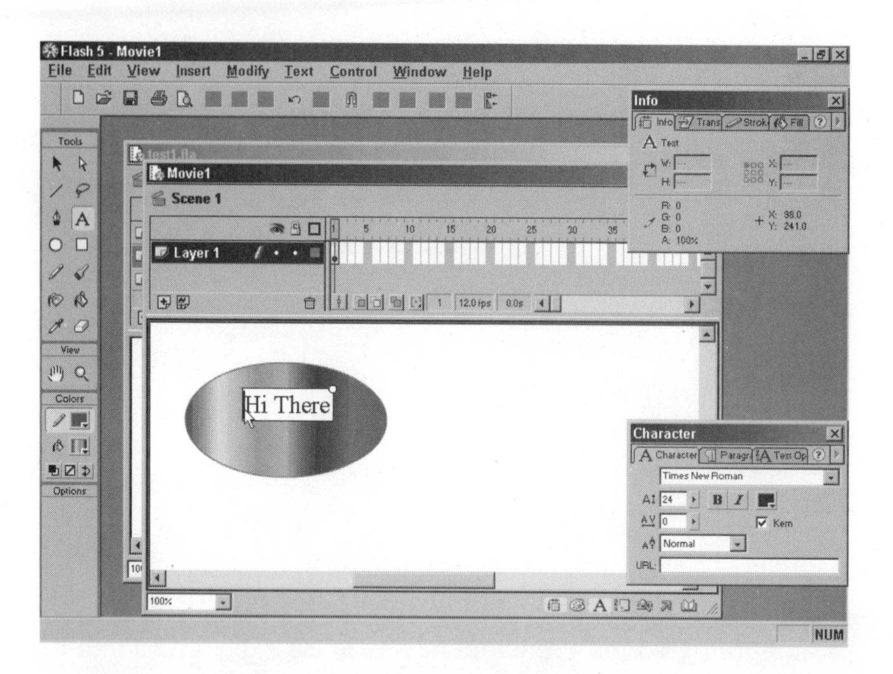

4. Select Edit ➢ Preferences, click the Clipboard tab, and click the arrow next to the Color Depth drop-down menu.

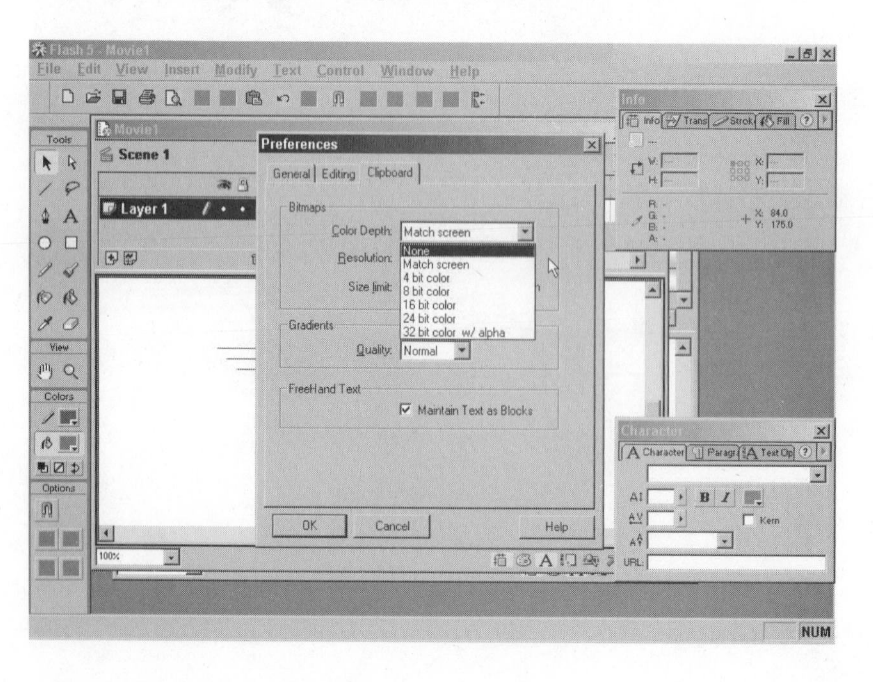

5. Select 4 Bit Color (this will diminish the color of the oval you drew). Click OK to close the Preferences window. Select your graphic by double-clicking it or drawing a box around it.

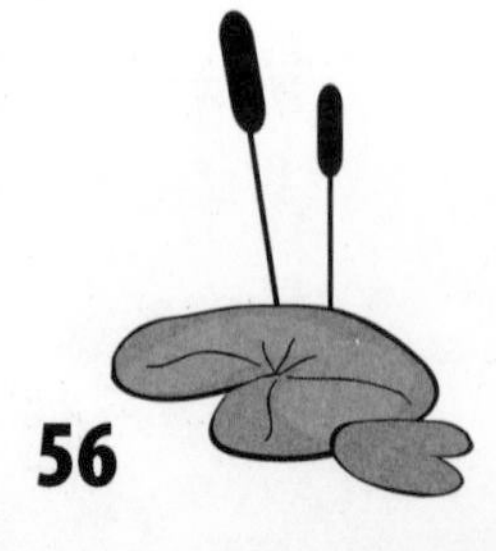

6. Click the Copy icon on the Toolbar, or select Edit ➢ Copy. This copies the graphic to the Clipboard.

7. Launch the Windows Paint program or the Mac Simple Text program. Select Paste from the Edit menu to view the bitmap you saved to the Clipboard.

8. Return to Flash and repeat steps 4 through 7, except this time, change the color depth to 24-bit color in step 5. Now view the results and notice the differences in quality and color. Although resolution is important to quality, it has nothing to do with color.

Note

Computer video quality is about 72 dpi (dots per inch), which is a poor resolution to use to print the document on a printer. The Color Depth setting has nothing to do with printing quality.

9. Click the arrow next to the Resolution drop-down menu. Leave the resolution at the Screen setting.

Note

Internet graphics are displayed at 72 dpi. A bitmap created and saved with a higher resolution will only have a larger file size and use more memory than one with a lower resolution. It will not appear to be higher quality.

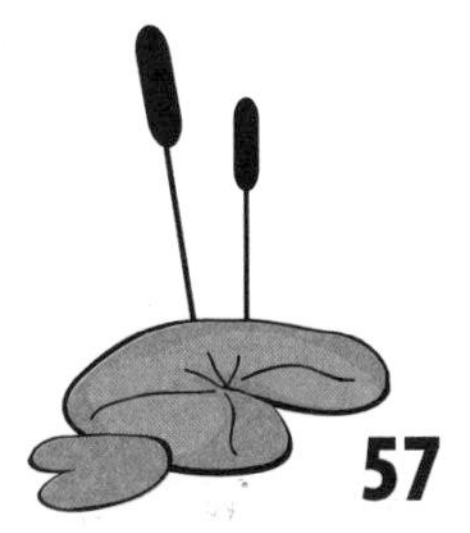

Note

The default setting for the bitmap size limit is 250 Kb (kilobytes). You may not need such a large graphic file if you are displaying it on the Web because, on the Web, the priority is how fast graphics display, and browsers download large files very slowly. On the other hand, you may want to edit your files in other programs that require larger files; in that case, you'll want the size limit to be larger.

antialiasing
A softening performed on the edges of a bitmap to result in a smoother appearance, most notable in curves and diagonal lines.

10. Check the Smooth check box to perform **antialiasing** on the bitmaps. This will dither (rearrange) the edges, resulting in a somewhat smoother picture.
11. Leave the Gradient Quality setting (only in Windows) at Normal. The Gradient Quality setting has no impact on graphics copied and pasted within Flash. It only affects those graphics copied from Flash and pasted into other applications in the Windows Metafile format.

Using Panels

panels
A series of windows, each with several tabs through which you can control specific actions or effects.

Panels are floating windows that can be moved around the work area or closed as needed. Each has several tabs that let you control specific actions or effects.

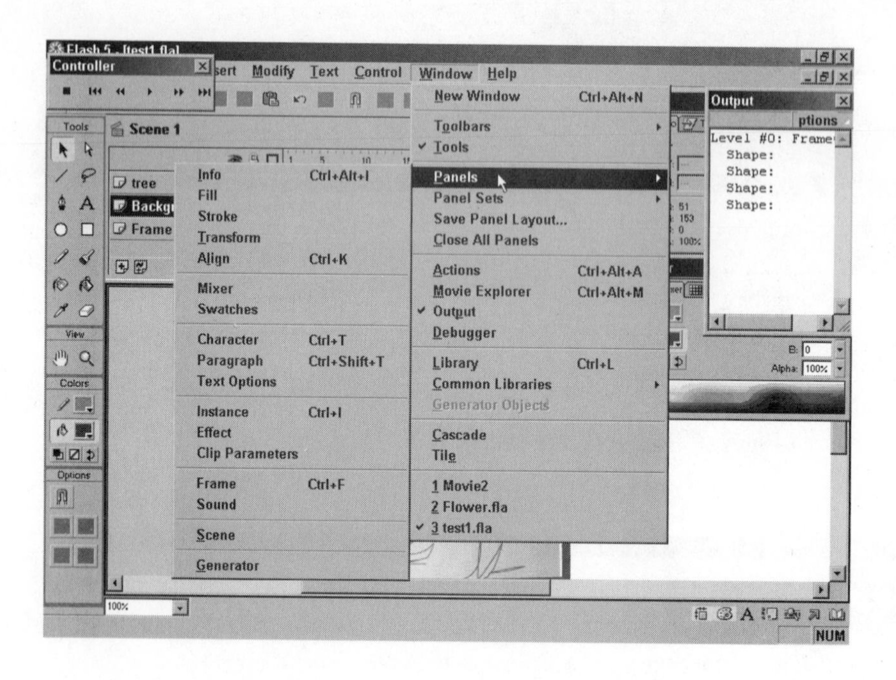

Transforming Objects and Determining Line and Fill Settings

One panel has separate menu tabs for Info, Transform, Stroke, and Fill:

1. Select Window ➢ Panel Sets ➢ Default Layout. The Info tab on the Info/Transform/Stroke/Fill Panel shows the size and coordinates of selected objects on the Stage.

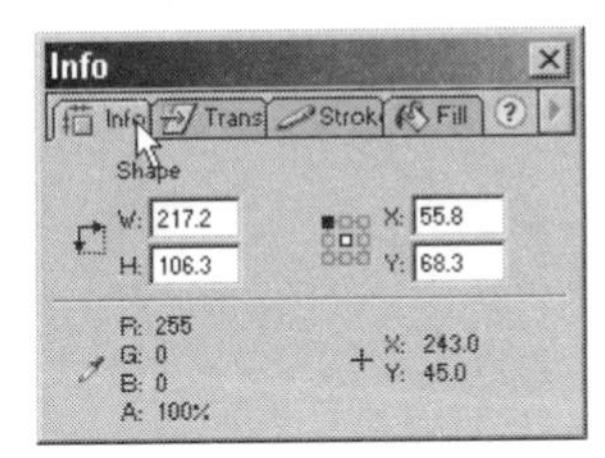

2. Click the Transform tab. Note that on this tab, you can scale, rotate, and skew your objects.

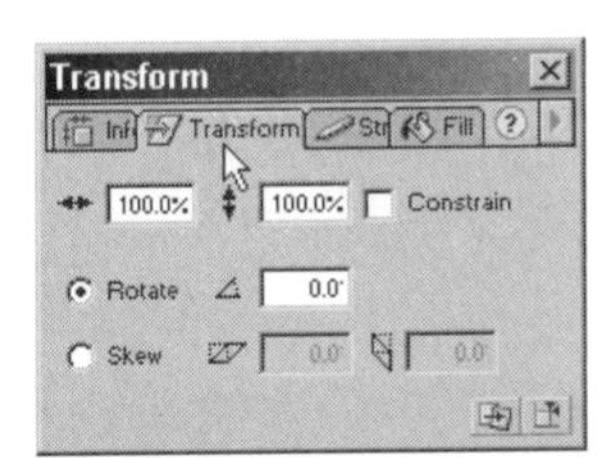

3. Select the Stroke tab. As you can see, you can use this tab to change the thickness and style of lines.

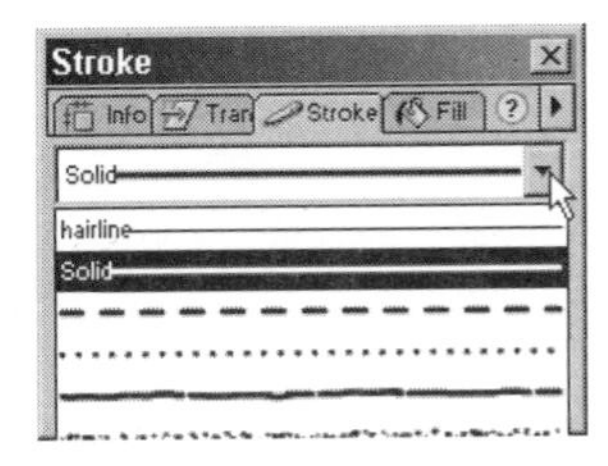

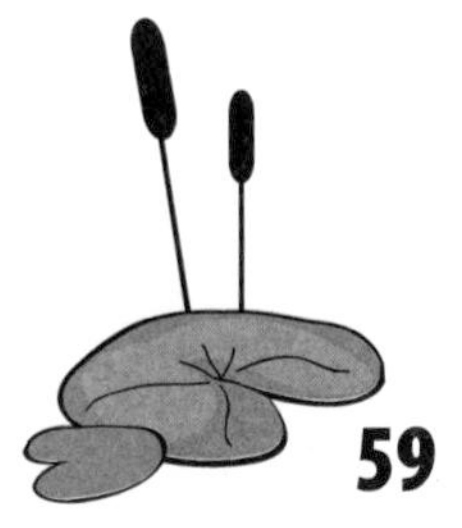

4. Select the Fill tab and click the Color button. The cursor turns into an eyedropper, which you can use to pick a color.

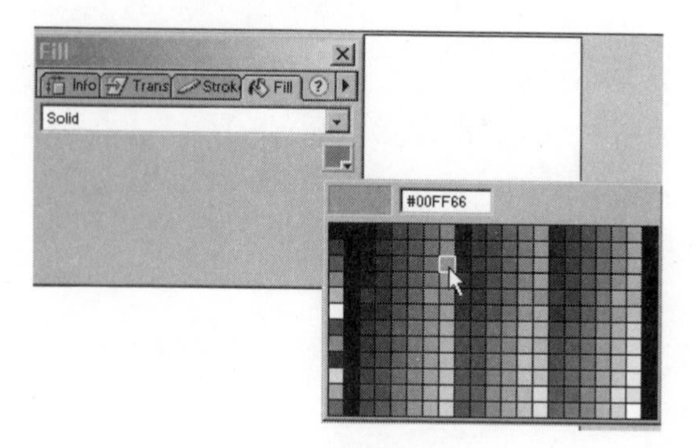

Mixing and Selecting Color

The Mixer panel contains both a color mixer and palette swatches. You can use the mixer boxes, labeled R, G and B, to mix different proportions of red, green, and blue to obtain new colors. Click the Swatches tab to see the color palette and the gradients available. You also can control the degree of transparency and opacity using the Alpha setting. One hundred percent on the Alpha setting is completely opaque and zero percent is completely transparent.

Tip

The menu tabs on the Mixer Panels (Mixer and Swatches) are also in the Colors box below the Toolbox.

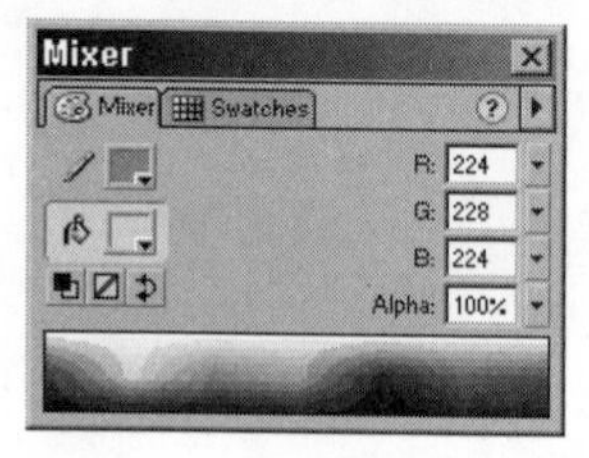

Setting Text Options

The Text Options panel includes Character, Paragraph, and Text Options menu tabs. You can use the Character tab to set font characteristics. The settings on

the Paragraph tab control how your text is formatted. The Text Options tab includes settings for static (regular) text, dynamic text, and input text. Dynamic text allows you to change text on the fly. Input text accepts user input in an input box or allows editing of text online.

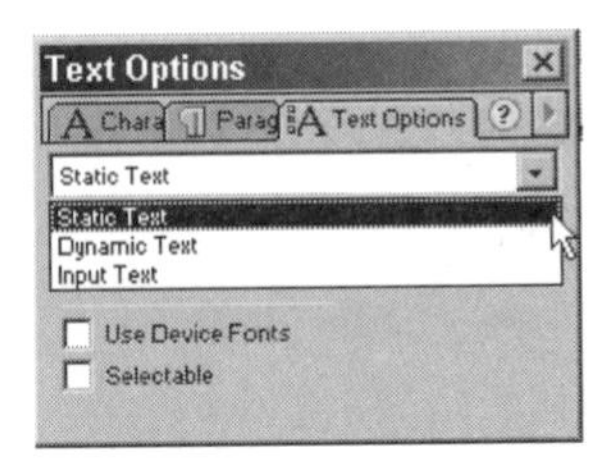

Managing Instances, Effects, Frames, and Sound

The Effect Panel provides options for working with instances, effects, frames, and sound. Select the Effect Panel and click the arrow next to the drop-down menu. Note the different effects you can set. You can modify the behavior and edit properties of instances of symbols from the Instance tab. The Effect tab is for adjusting color tint, brightness, and degree of transparency. On the Frame tab, you can create a label for the instance and determine the type of animation (None means that there is no animation). The Sound tab lets you select the sound file from a list of imported files (if there is more than one). You can create sound effects such as fading sound in and out and switching the sound from one channel to another. You also can synchronize the sound to events on a timeline.

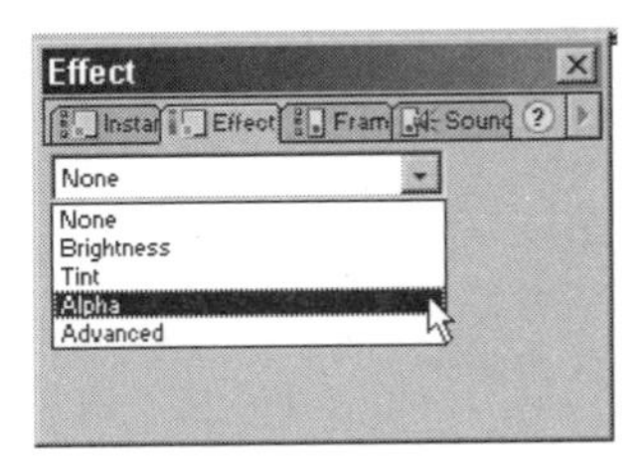

Note

Window ➢ Close All Panels clears all panels but does not affect the objects on the Stage.

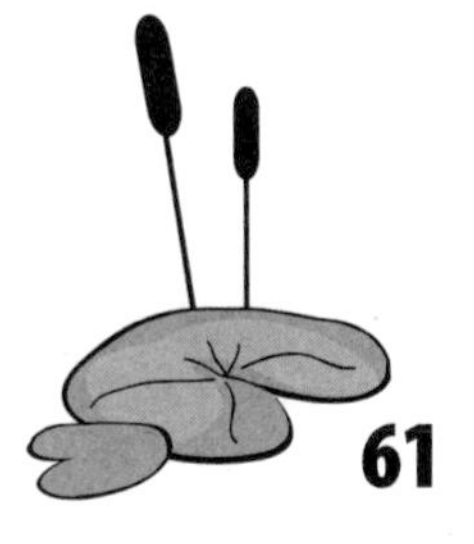

Saving Panel Layouts

Once you have begun a movie project and determined which panels you are going to use frequently, you can save the layout:

1. Select Window ➢ Panel Sets ➢ Default Layout.

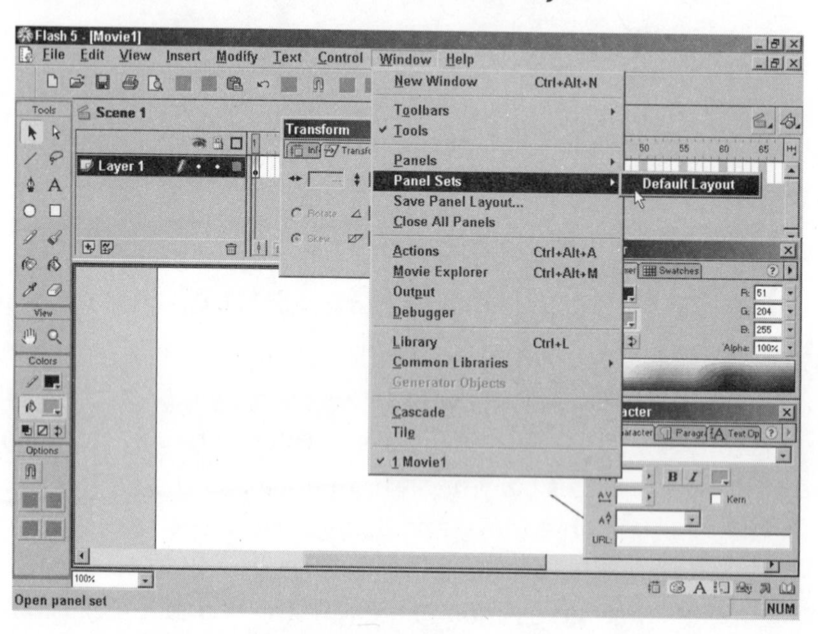

2. Click the Close button on the Info/Transform/Stroke/Fill Panel window.
3. Select Window ➢ Save Panel Layout. Enter **Project1** in the Save Panel Layout dialog box and click OK. The panel layout will be saved under that name.

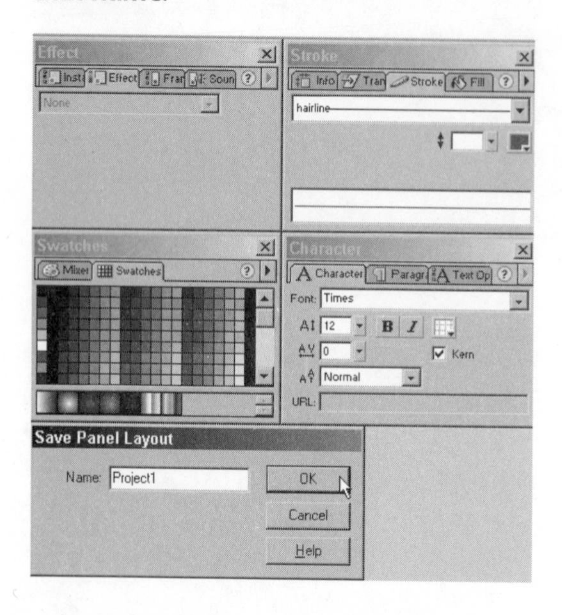

4. Select Window ➢ Panel Sets ➢ Project1. Notice that Project1 is now available for selection.

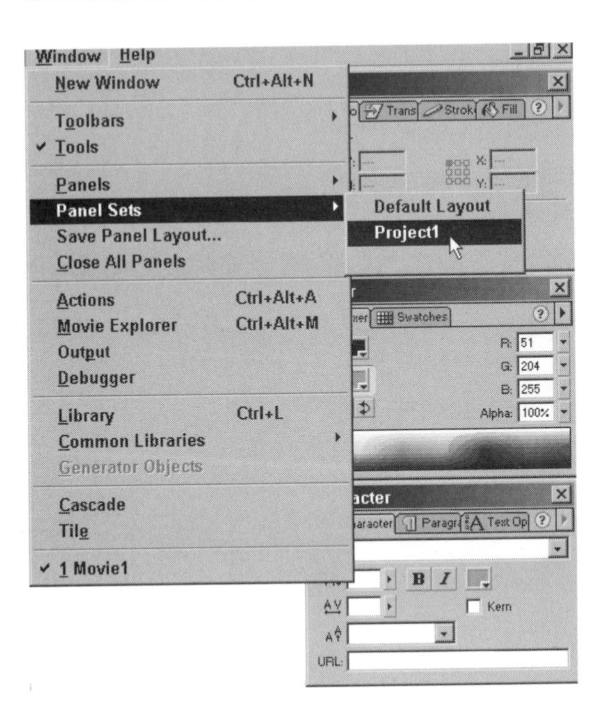

What's Next?

Now that you have learned about many of the menu functions and preferences settings, you will be able to draw on this information to develop exciting movies.

Part 2

Creating in Flash

Now that you've had an introduction to the tools, it's time to start using them. In this section, you will learn to draw and paint through some beginning exercises in Chapter 3. In Chapter 4, you'll create symbols that you can then re-use in your Web sites. Chapter 5 teaches you how to manipulate text in Flash. Finally, Chapter 6 introduces you to layers.

Creating in Flash

Chapter 3

Drawing and Painting in Flash

You have already had a glimpse of how much is possible with the drawing and painting tools in Flash. When you begin drawing and painting on the Stage, you will see that practically the only limit will be your imagination. In this chapter, you will draw, shape, and paint a house to learn the ins and outs of Flash's powerful tools.

- Drawing with the Line Tools
- Combining Tools to Enhance Your Drawing
- Using the Painting Tools

Drawing with the Line Tools

The line tools include the **Line tool**, the **Pencil tool**, and the **Pen tool**. Each has something unique to contribute to your effort. Figuring out just which tool and which modifiers to use in a specific situation is the challenge.

Line tool
Use the Line tool to draw straight lines. To use it, click a starting point, move the mouse, and then click an ending point. The line will be drawn between the two points.

Pencil tool
Use the Pencil for freehand drawing. You can determine the shape and trajectory of the line by using the Straighten, Smooth, and Ink tool modifiers in the Options box.

Pen tool
Use the Pen tool to draw straight lines and curves. It draws along a Bezier path. To draw lines, click to start, move the cursor to an ending point for the line, then click to draw the line between the two points. To make more segments, move to a new ending point and click. To begin new line segments, double-click on the existing line. You can make curves by dragging before releasing the mouse button.

Setting Up the Drawing

A good way to learn how to use new tools is to have a purpose for using them. Starting a new project with a goal in mind is an excellent way to begin. Your goal here is to build a house with the drawing tools. First, you must set up your drawing:

1. Launch Flash and save your movie using File ➢ Save As. Name the movie "House."

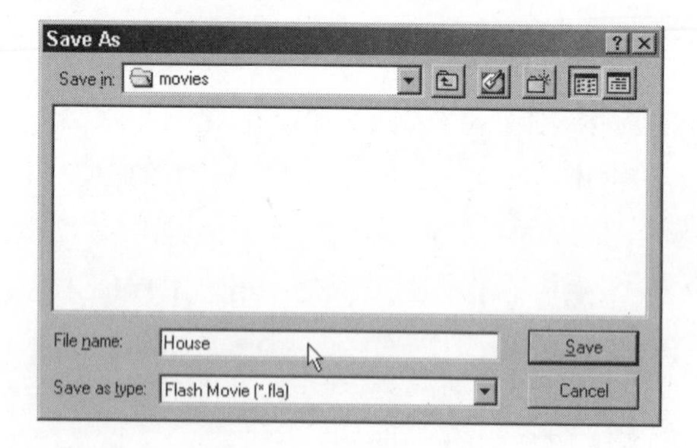

Tip

When you save a file, Flash appends the `.fla` extension to the filename.

2. It will help you draw if you have guidelines. To add guidelines to your drawing, select View ➢ Rulers; rulers will appear on the top and left side of the Stage.

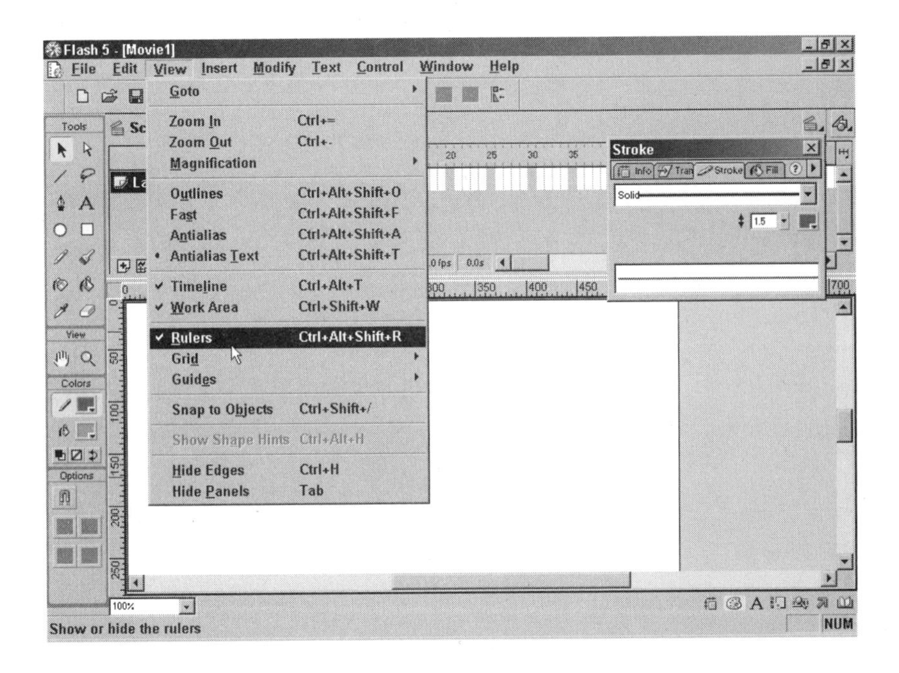

3. Select View ➢ Grid ➢ Show Grid. The rulers and grid will provide support when you draw your house.

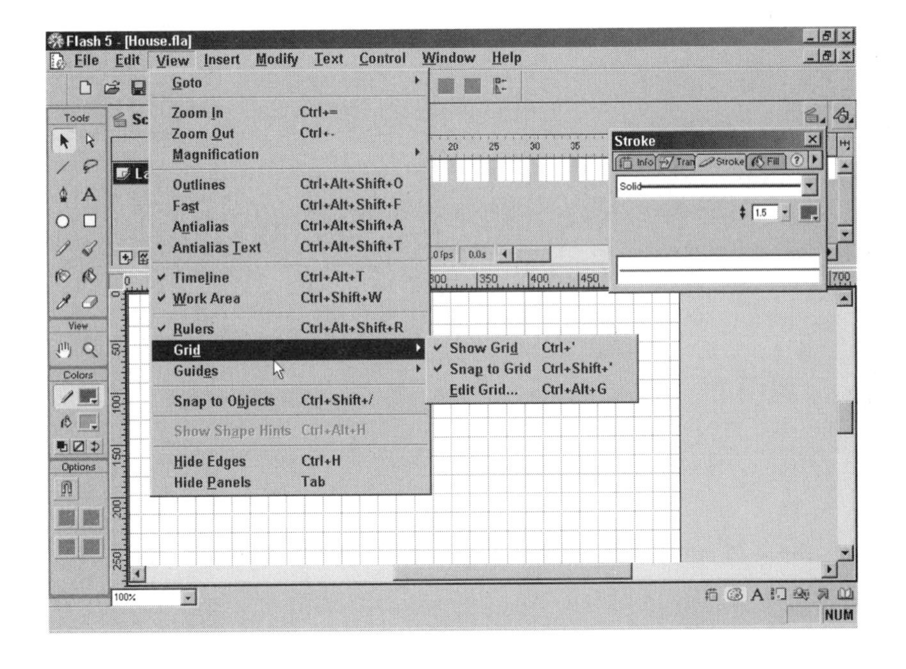

Drawing a House

Let's start with the Pencil tool to create some of the features of the house:

1. Select the Pencil tool and the Straighten option and then draw a box on the Stage. Use the scroll bars to move the ruler origin points as shown.

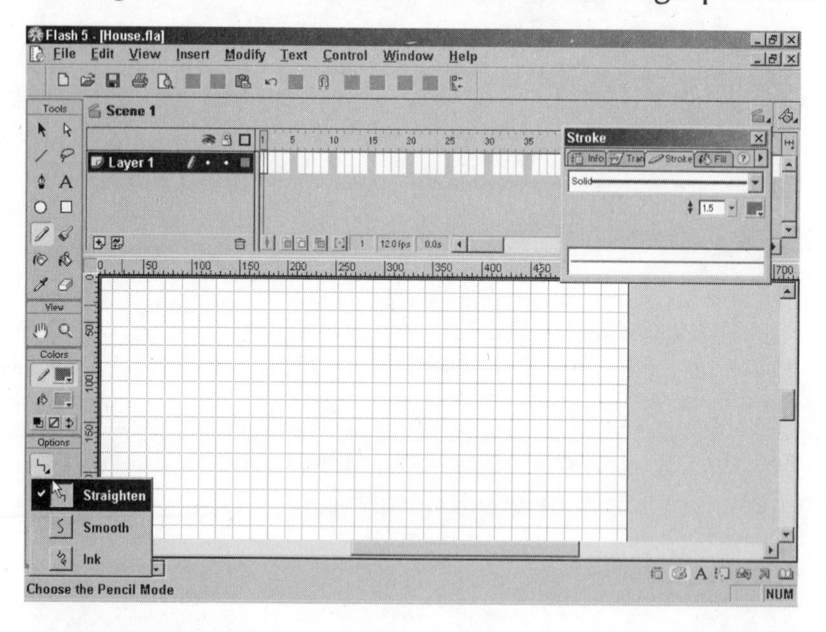

2. Start the drawing in the upper-left corner at about the 150-unit mark on the vertical ruler and the 50-unit mark on the horizontal ruler. It's great that even a crude attempt at drawing a box will result in a square with straight lines when you use the Straighten option.

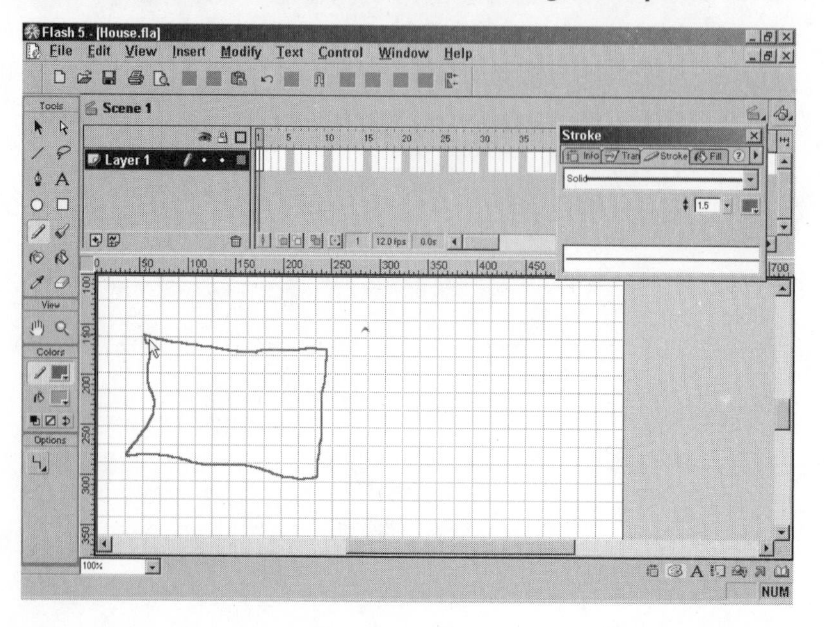

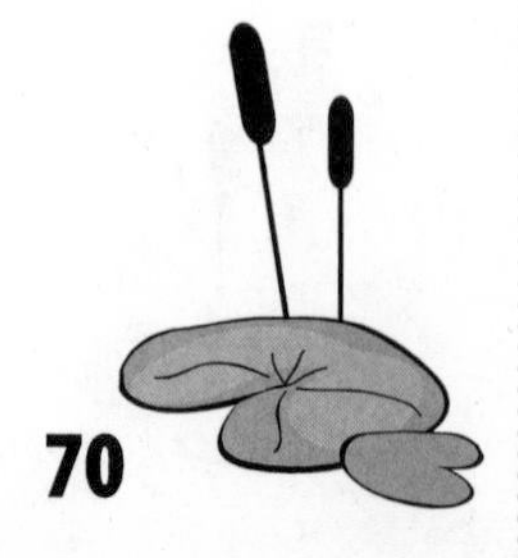

3. Using the Pencil tool, draw a small window on the left side of the house and a large window on the right side. Draw a front door and a step in front of it. Notice how easily the lines snap to the grid. The step will appear in perspective; you will see the front and top.

Tip

Select Edit ➢ Undo if you make a mistake.

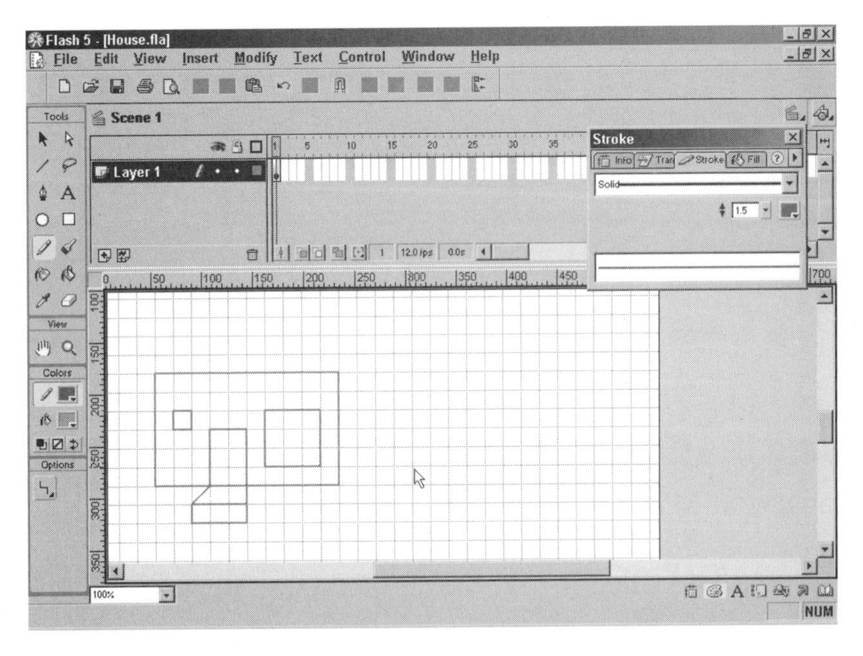

Drawing the Roof with the Line Tool

Now let's use the Line tool to draw the roof:

1. Select the Line tool. Determine the midpoint of the house. Begin at the midpoint about 50 units above the house and draw a line from the roof peak to just beyond the edge of the house on one side. Repeat this from the roof peak to the edge on the other side. Complete the roof by using the Line tool to close up the roofline.

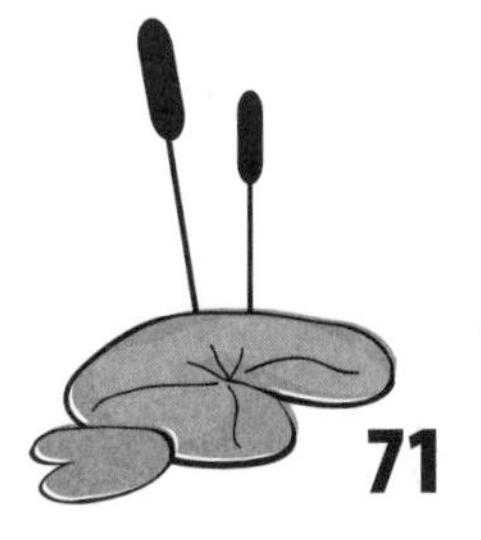

2. Add a chimney with either the Line or Pencil tool. Draw a sloped vertical line from the roof peak to the top of the house.

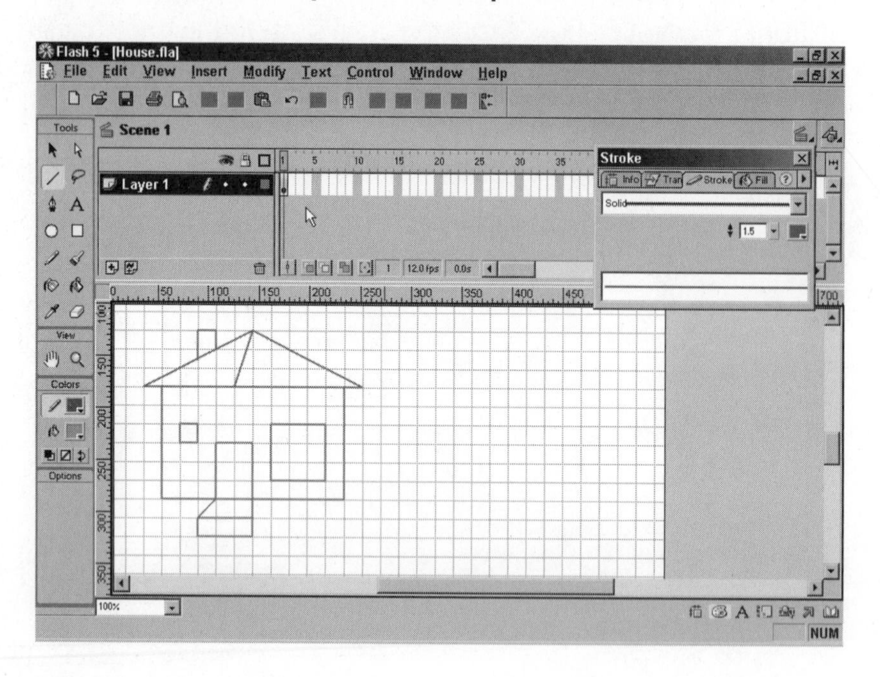

Drawing the Roof with the Pen Tool

Alternatively, you can use the Pen tool to draw the roofline:

1. Use the Arrow tool to select each line segment of the roof and press the Delete key to erase.
2. Select the Pen tool and click at a point on the lower-left edge of the housetop. Position the Pen at a point where the roof peak should be and click. Release the button, move to the opposite edge of the roof, and click. You should now have the upper portion of the roof.
3. Carefully click just at the roof peak. Move the mouse to a point in the middle of the housetop and click to make a nearly vertical line as shown.

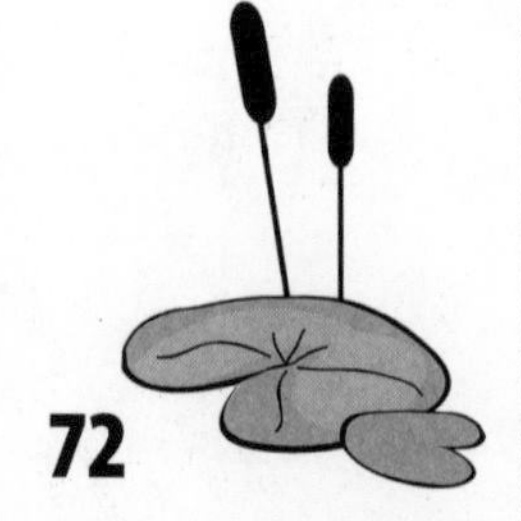

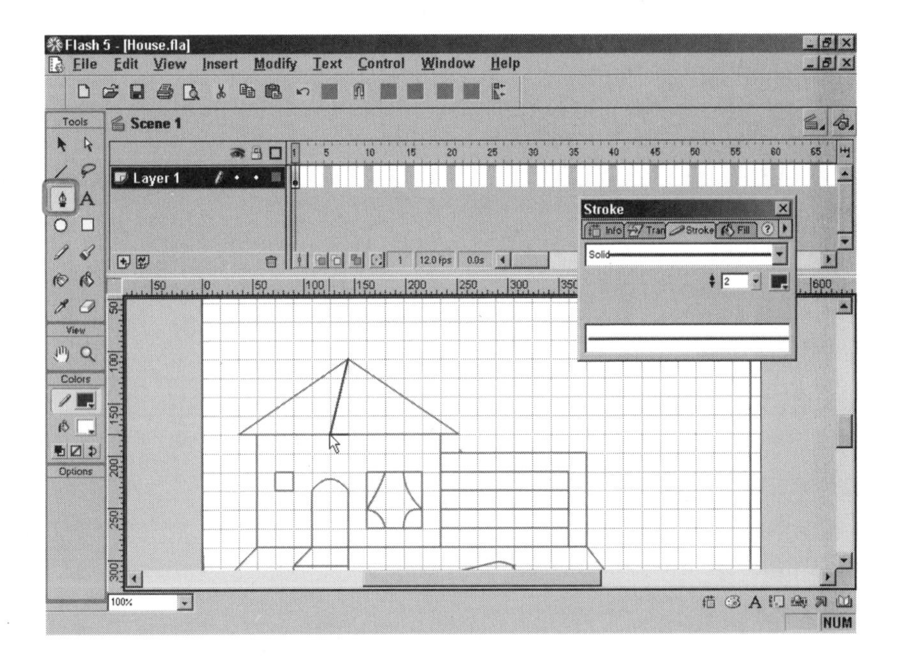

Drawing Curtains and a Doorknob with the Pencil Tool

You are going to add a couple of features to give the house a more homey appearance:

1. Use the Pencil to dress up the house with curtains. Select the Smooth or Ink mode (rather than the Straighten mode) for this task. Add other accessories and draw a garage next to the house.

Tip

When you make a mistake you can select Edit ➢ Undo as many times as you specified under Edit ➢ Preferences. The default is 100.

2. It can be easier to draw freehand with the grid turned off. The Snap to Grid menu option is an option that can be toggled on and off. If it's on (checked), you can turn it off by choosing View ➢ Grid ➢ Snap to Grid. Using the Pencil tool, draw a doorknob. Try the doorknob with Snap to Grid turned on. Use Undo to restore your old doorknob. Turn Snap to Grid back off.

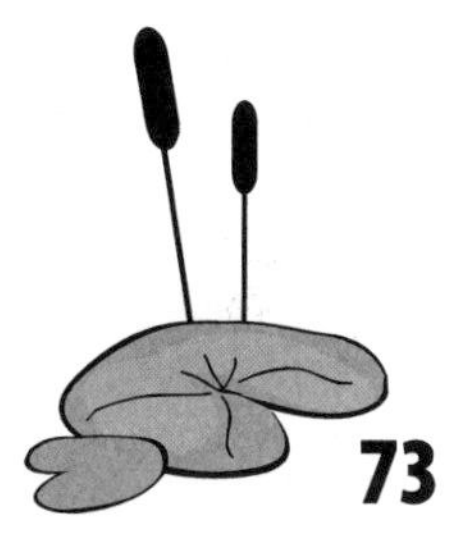

Modifying Lines

Lines are easy to modify. Because you can use most of the tools to change lines (the Line tool, the Pencil tool, the Pen tool, the Subselect tool, the Ink Bottle tool, and the Arrow tool), there are countless variations on the types of lines you can use in a drawing.

Arrow tool
Use the Arrow tool to select and modify objects. You can click to select a segment of an object and double-click to select the entire object. You can manipulate lines by pulling them while clicking and dragging.

Creating an Arch with the Arrow Tool

With the **Arrow tool**, you can manipulate lines by pulling them while clicking and dragging. While the Arrow tool is touching a line, either a right angle symbol (it looks like a corner) or an arc symbol will appear below the cursor. The angle means that if you drag the line at that point, it will pull into a straight angle, and the arc signifies that with any manipulation, the line will take the form of a rounded line.

Let's use the Arrow tool to add an arch to the doorway. Move the cursor to the middle of the top of the doorway. With the cursor touching the line across the top of the door, look for the arc below the arrow and then pull the line into an arch. If your line gets out of shape, just select Edit ➢ Undo and try again.

Tip

Some of the maneuvers with the Arrow tool require the precision that comes only with practice using the mouse. Practice on a blank Stage by creating a new movie, or use an area on the Stage away from your work.

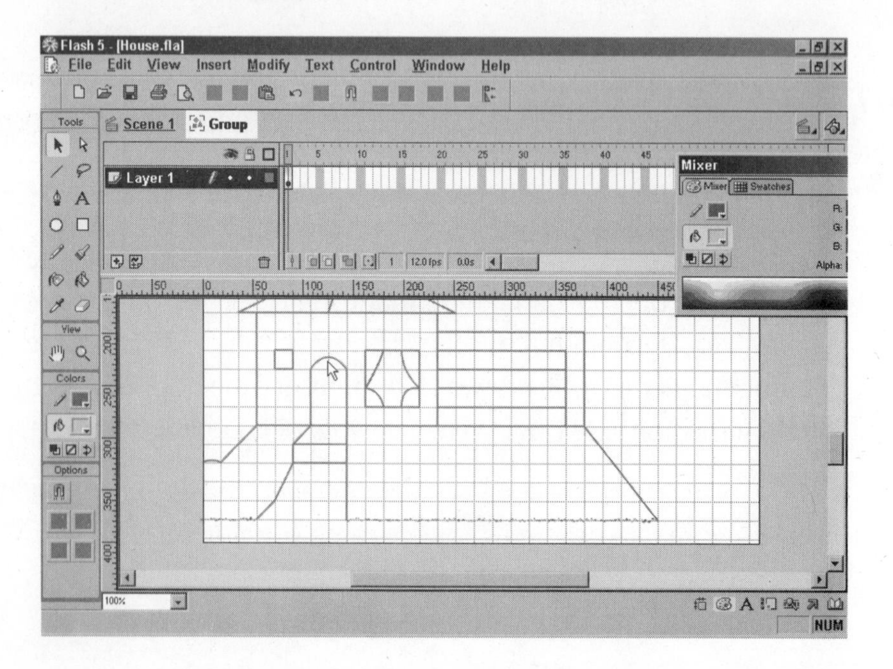

Creating a Lawn with the Pencil Tool

A grassy border would be a nice touch for the front walk. You can use the Pencil tool to create the effect:

1. Select the Pencil tool and change the line color to a shade of green.
2. Select Window ➢ Panels ➢ Stroke. Click the down arrow on the line style menu and pick the broken line style that resembles grass.
3. Click the arrow on the Stroke width drop-down and change the width to 3 points. Draw a line across the front of the property, leaving a space for the walkway. If you want, erase the line from the step to the street and replace it with the broken line.

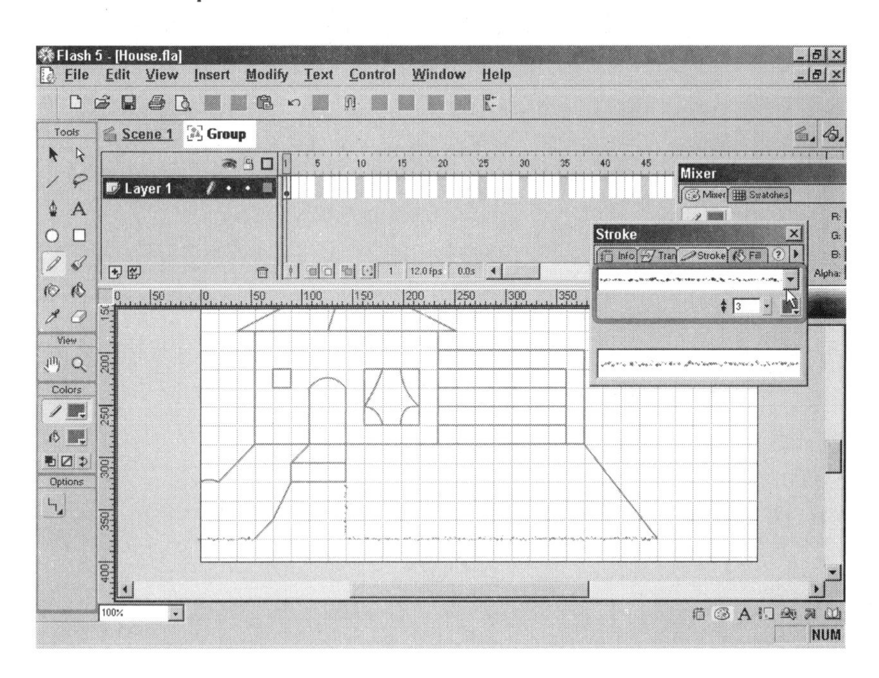

Combining Tools to Enhance your Drawing

Lines are naturally more interesting when combined with shapes than they are alone because both can be used to create more sophisticated objects. You can add the selection tools to design some amazing scenes.

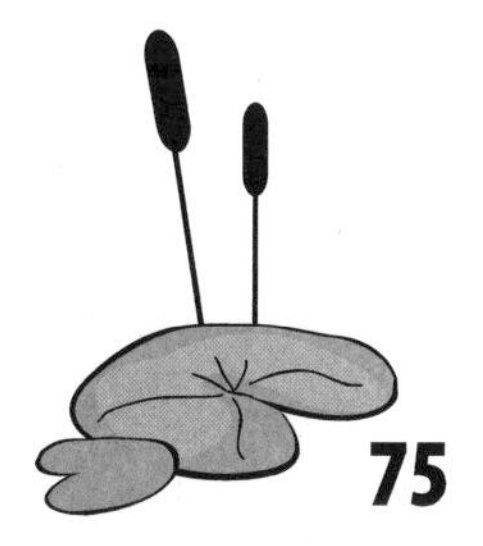

Understanding Object Interaction

When objects come in contact with one another on the same layer, they make a connection so that the object on the top displaces the portion of the bottom object that it covers. Thus, when you move the top object, the underneath portion of the bottom object disappears.

Next, you'll experiment with drawing shapes to see how they interact:

1. Click File ➢ New to get a new drawing area. Leave the House file on the Stage.
2. Select the **Oval tool** and draw two ovals side by side.

Oval tool

Use the Oval tool to draw circles and oval shapes. You can fill the shape once it's drawn.

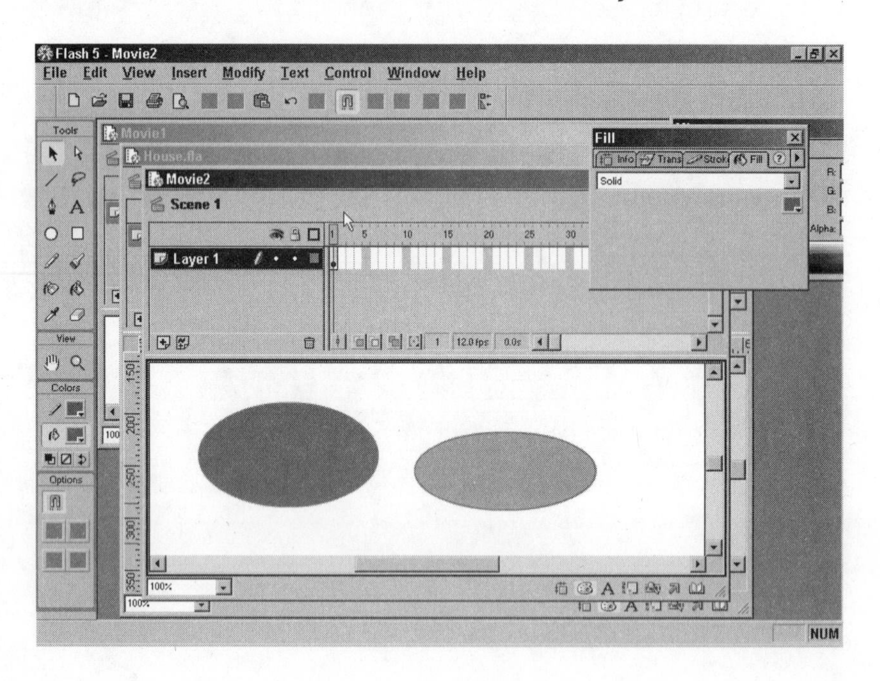

3. Select the second oval and drag it onto the first oval so that they overlap.
4. Deselect the oval you moved, then reselect it and move it away from the first oval.

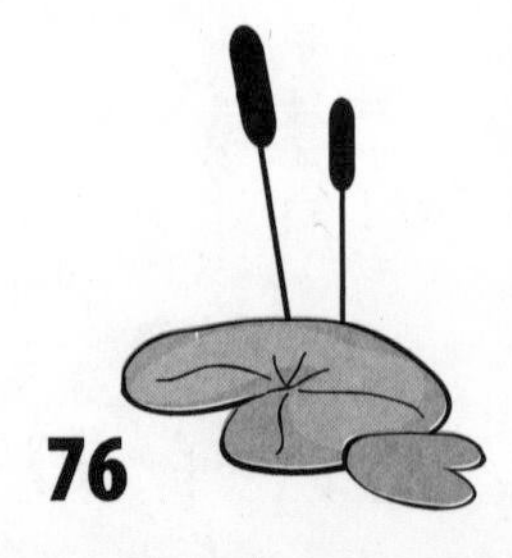

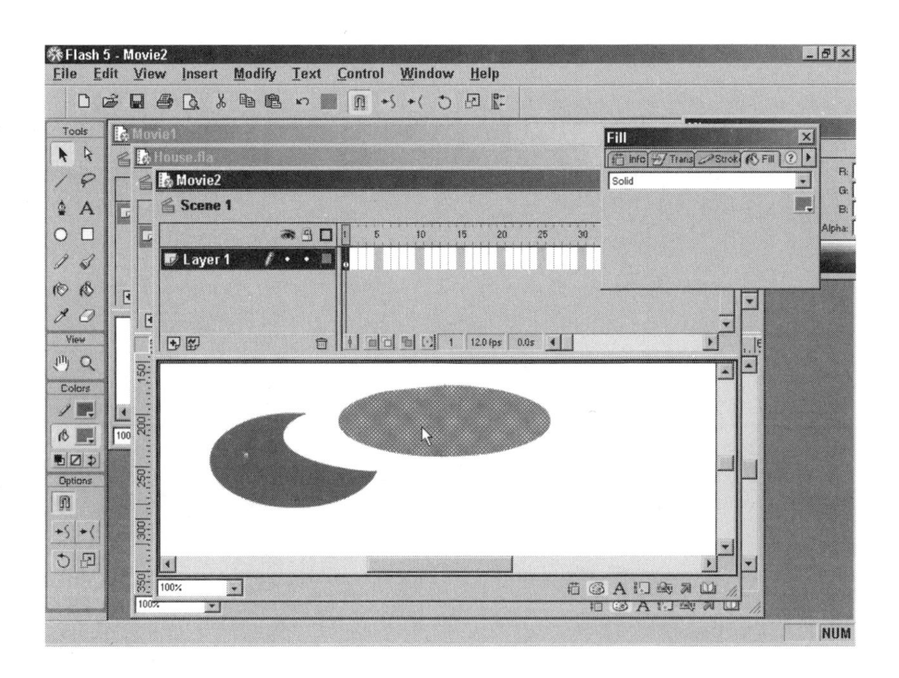

Grouping Objects

When you intersect lines and shapes, they become linked and cannot be separated into their original parts. The solution is to **group** objects that you want to remain independent from other objects. You also can combine more than one object into a group. Let's group some objects in the house to create other objects:

1. Because one oval seems to have taken a chunk out of the other oval, select Edit ➢ Undo to undo the last step.
2. Draw two new ovals. Select an oval with the Arrow tool or double-click on the object. Select Modify ➢ Group to create a group of the shape and border.

group
Use Modify ➢ Group to combine two or more selected objects. Once a group is formed, its objects cannot be connected to other objects. Any modification will be to the entire group. Groups can be broken apart by selecting Modify ➢ Break Apart.

Note

You can select an object by drawing a box around it using the Arrow tool or by double-clicking it while using the Arrow tool. Clicking only once will select only the fill or the line, but not both.

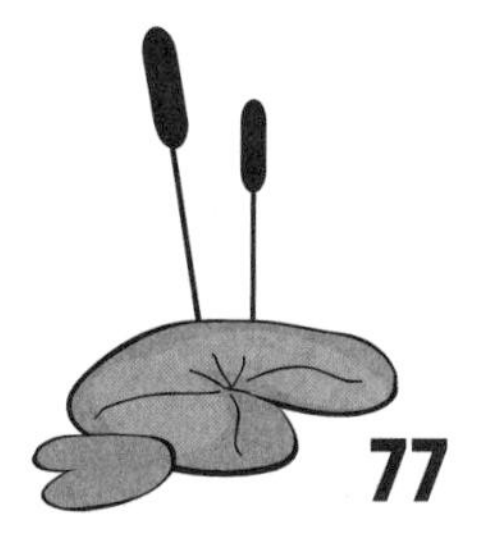

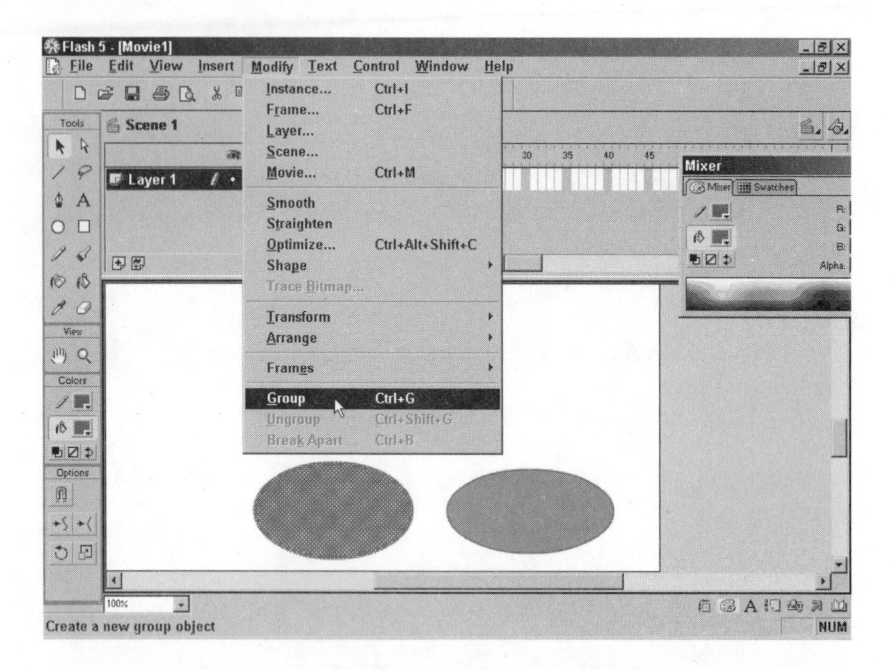

3. Select the ungrouped oval and drag it onto the grouped one.

4. Deselect and then select the ungrouped oval and pull it away.

Now the first oval retains its shape. Notice also that the second oval moves underneath the grouped oval rather than on top.

Note

When you create a group, the group is placed at the top of the stacking order of all objects.

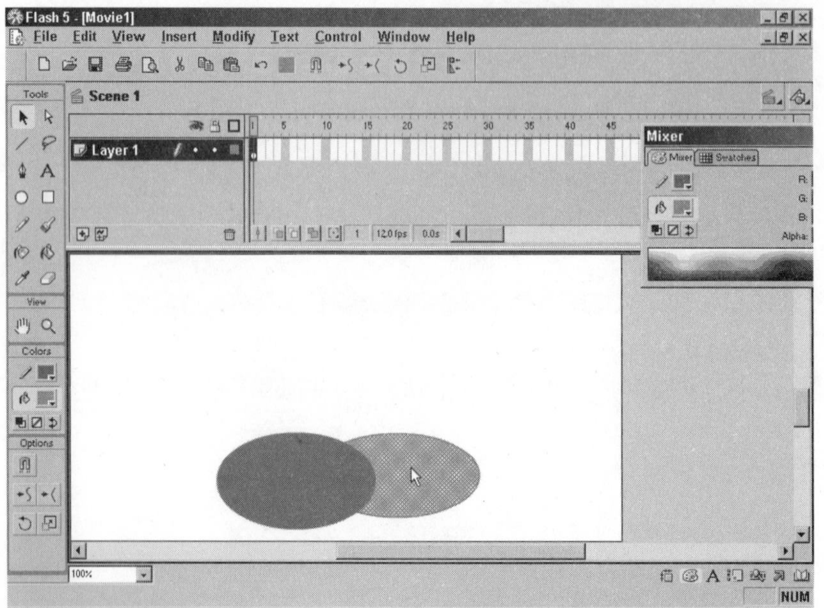

Creating a Lawnmower

You can make some enhancements, such as adding some garden implements, to your house by using shapes and lines together. Sometimes objects should be grouped to preserve their integrity and to facilitate combining them with other objects.

Using the Rectangle Tool to Draw the Lawnmower

Let's place a lawnmower on the house's front lawn:

1. Select Window ➢ Panels ➢ Fill and then select None from the drop-down menu.

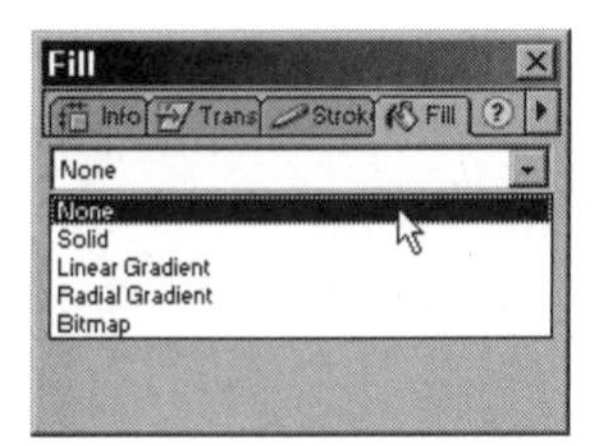

2. Select the **Rectangle tool** and then click the Rectangle Radius modifier in the Options box.

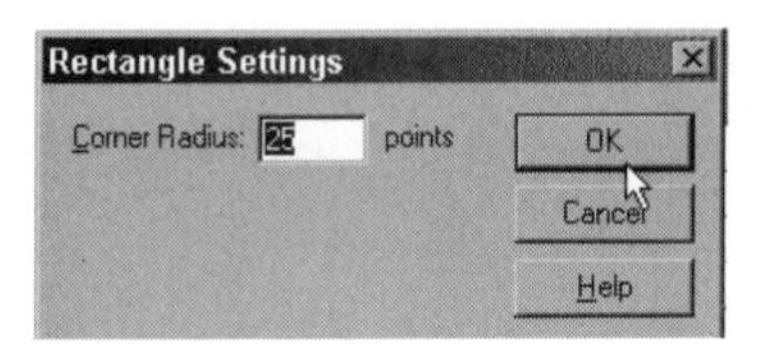

3. Change the Corner Radius setting to 25 points and click OK.

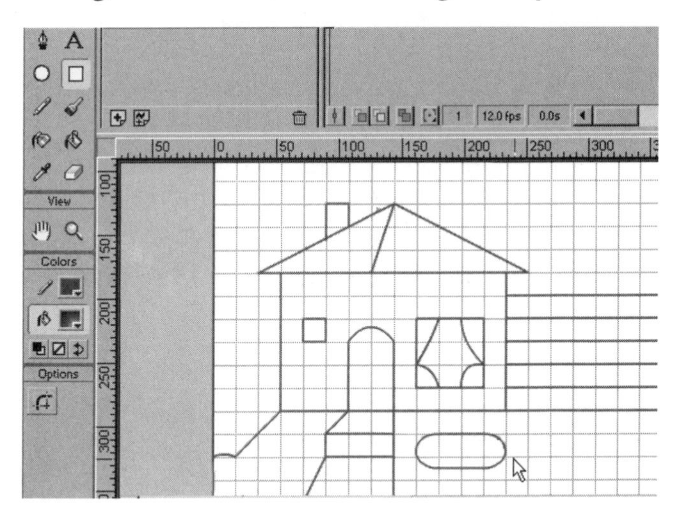

Rectangle tool

Use the Rectangle tool to draw squares and rectangles. You can use the Radius modifier in the Options box to round the corners. The rectangle can be filled; when it is first drawn, it will be filled with the default color.

Subselect tool

You can use the Subselect tool to drag and reshape, much like you use the Arrow tool. When you select Subselect and then select an object, handles are displayed on the object. You can change the shape of the object by clicking and dragging the handles.

Lasso tool

The Lasso tool enables you to select areas by drawing a boundary around them. When you want to draw a straight selection area, use the Polygon modifier, and to draw a free-hand selection area, use the Magic Wand. The Polygon and Magic Wand modifiers are modifiers to the Lasso tool and are located in the Options box.

As you'll recall from Chapter 1, the selection tools are the Arrow (cursor), the **Subselect tool**, and the **Lasso tool**. You will make use of these tools, along with the other shape and line tools you have learned about in this chapter, to add more to the house you have already created.

Scaling and Rotating with the Arrow Tool

You have been using the Arrow tool to move and select areas of your work, but you have not made use of its scaling and rotating features. Let's use Scale and Rotate to adjust the size and orientation of objects. The handles that display on the side of the rectangle will stretch the object, whereas the corner handles will make the object larger or smaller in proportion. This adjustment is important to make objects in your drawing more realistic:

1. Draw a round corner rectangle on the lawn near the front step. Select the Arrow tool, then double-click the round corner rectangle you just drew. Select the Scale icon in the Options box below the Toolbox or the toolbar. The small squares that form on the rectangle can be used to stretch or shrink the shape or to distort it. Flatten the rectangle a little by clicking and dragging to pull the top line down a little.

Tip

You also can use the Copy and Paste options from the Edit menu or the toolbar to duplicate an object.

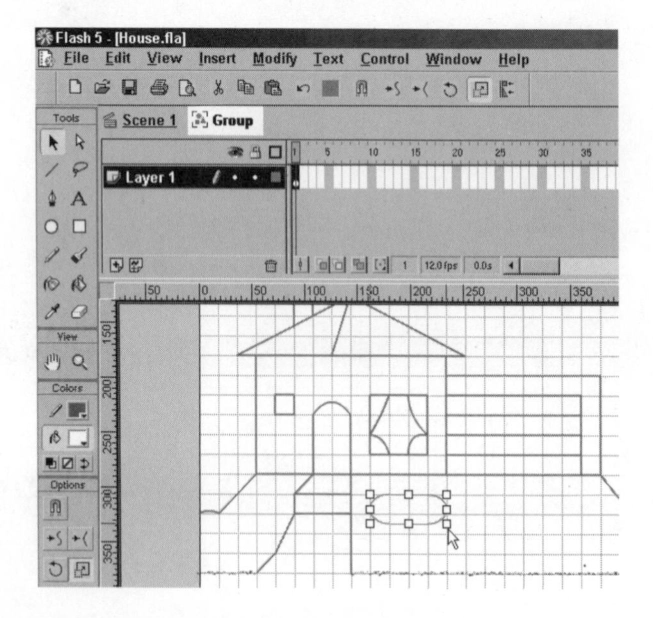

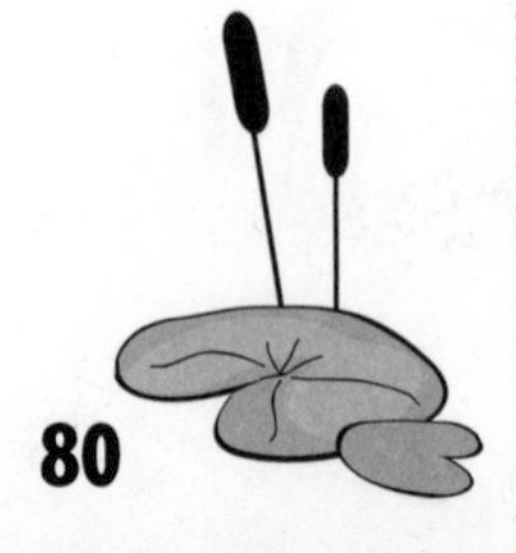

2. Select the Oval tool and draw a small circle to create a wheel.

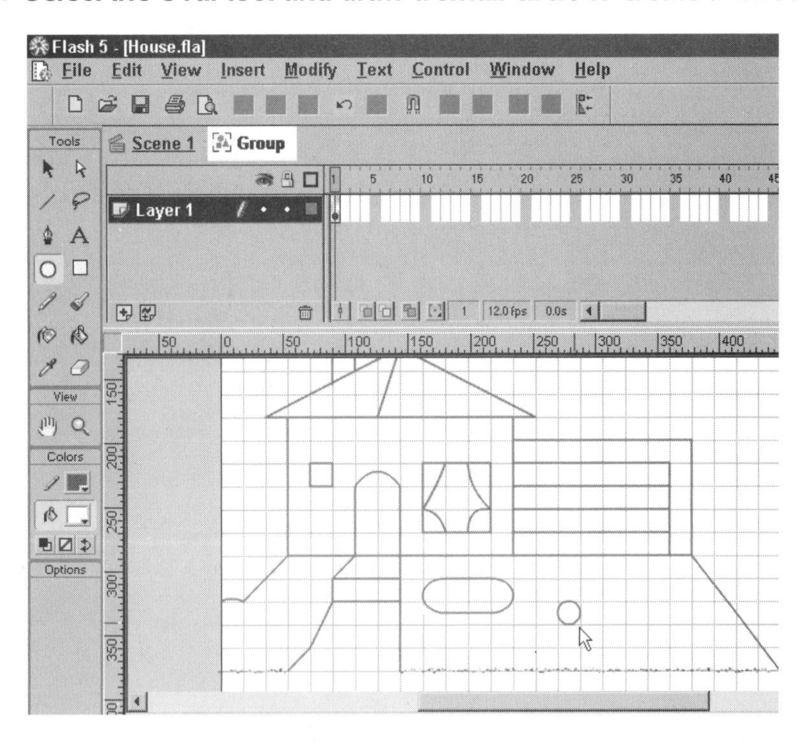

3. Select the wheel and then select Edit ➢ Duplicate to make another wheel exactly like the first.

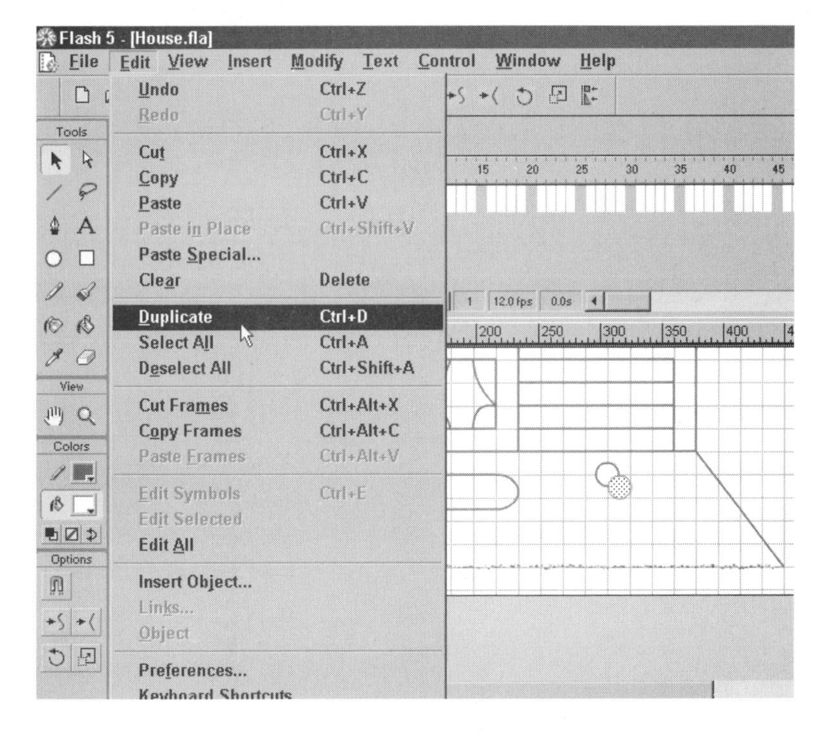

4. Position the wheels along the bottom of the rectangle, like lawn-mower wheels. Select the rectangle and the two wheels. Select Modify ➢ Group to make them a group. This will prevent the handle from attaching when it overlaps the body of the mower.

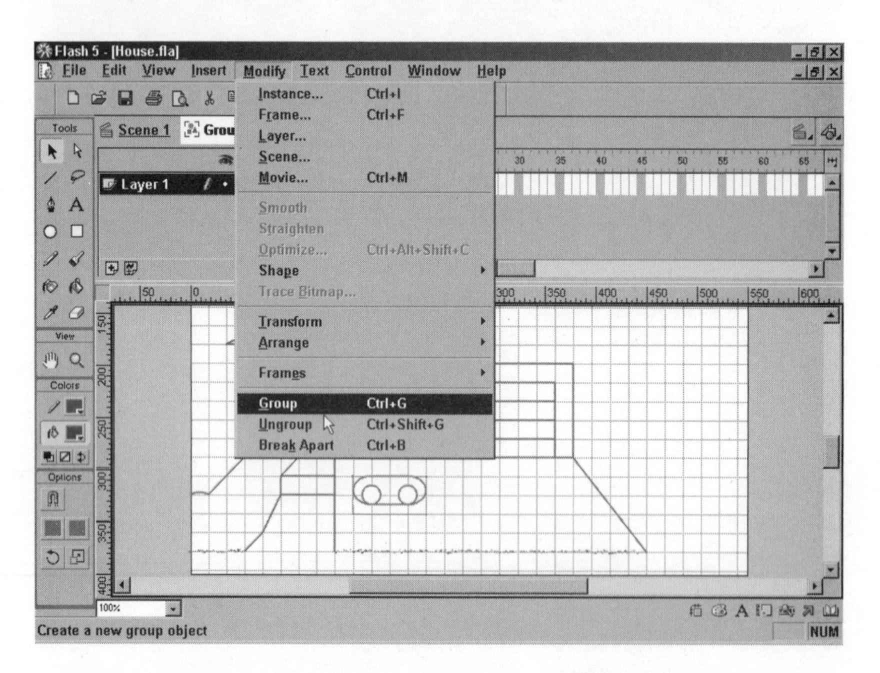

5. Select the Oval tool once again and draw the handle for the mower. Select the handle using the Arrow cursor and select the Rotate modifier from the Options box or from the toolbar. Rotate the handle so that it is slightly higher on the end. Deselect the handle when you are satisfied with its angle.

Note

When you choose the Scale option to use with a selected object, the object handles are square. When you choose the Rotate option for a selected object, the object handles are round.

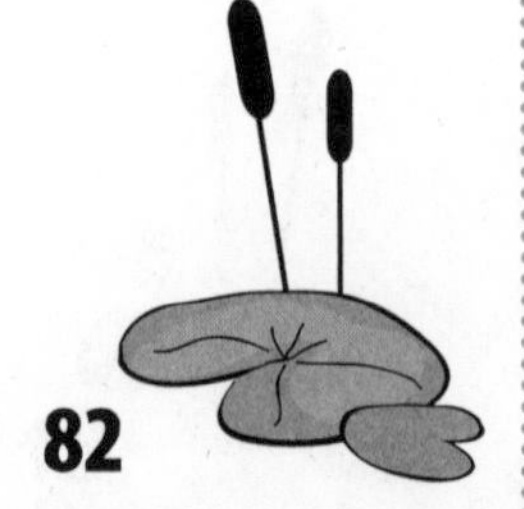

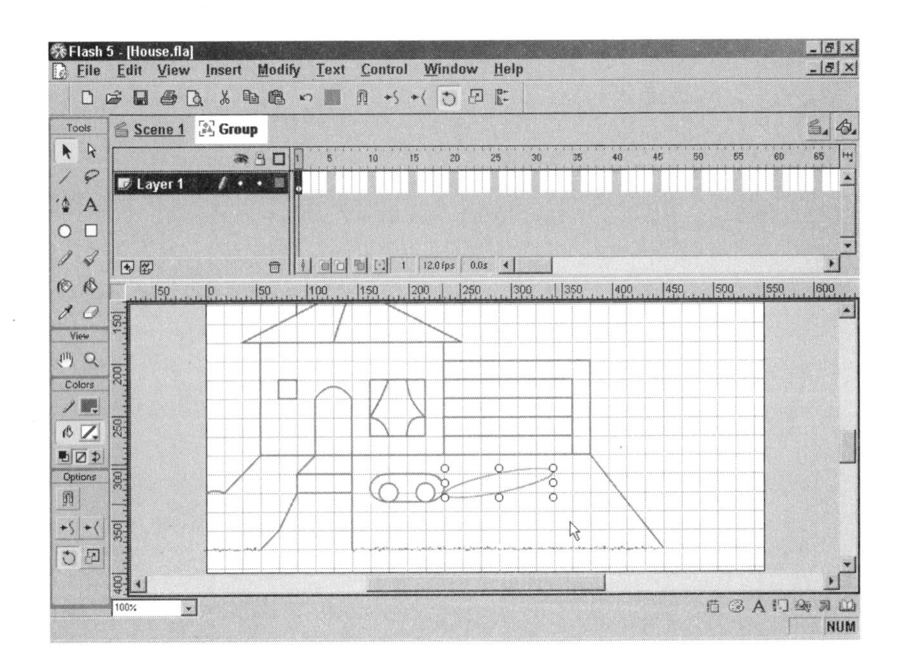

6. Place the Arrow cursor over one end of the handle without selecting the handle. Notice the small arc below the arrow. This indicates that you can pull the line in an arc shape. Squash, rather than pull, the handle so that it flattens a little. Repeat the same procedure on the other end so that it resembles a mower handle, and then select it and push toward the mower body until it looks like it's attached.

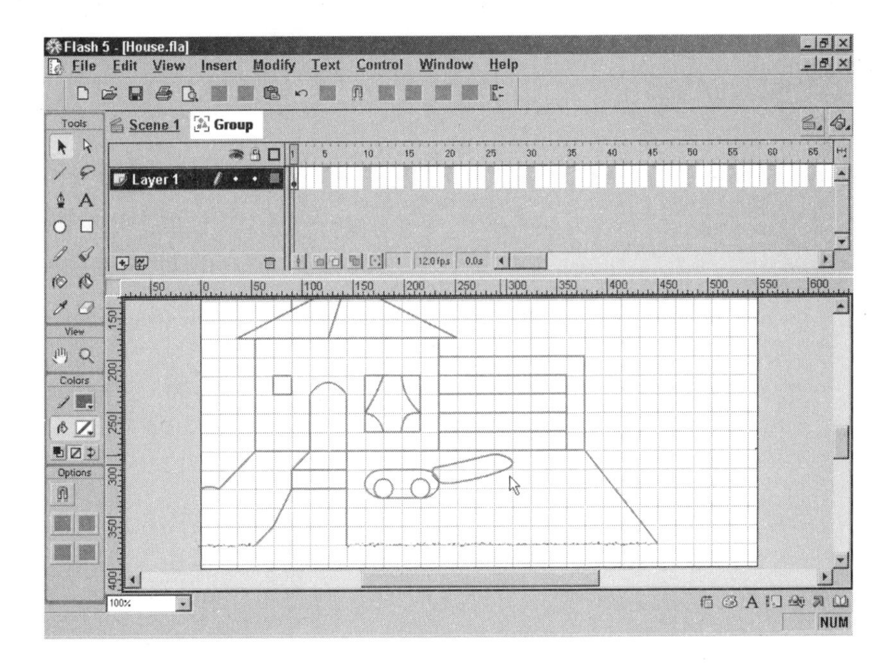

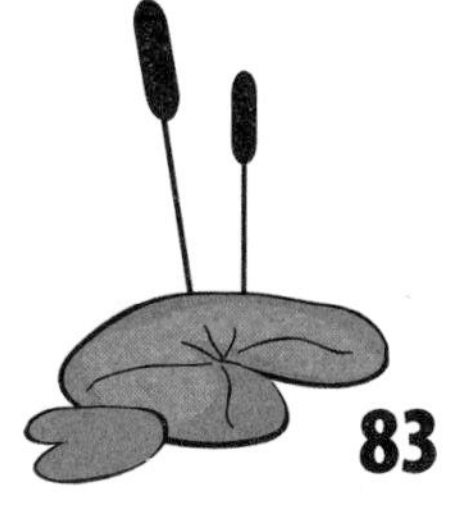

Dragging and Reshaping with the Subselect Tool

You can use the Subselect tool to drag and reshape. When you select it and then select an object, the Subselect tool displays handles on the object. You can click and drag the handles to change the shape of the object. Let's try it:

1. Select the Subselect tool and select the mower handle.
2. Use the mouse to grab one of the handles at the center of the upper portion of the handle. Pull in the desired direction to create a better-shaped handle.

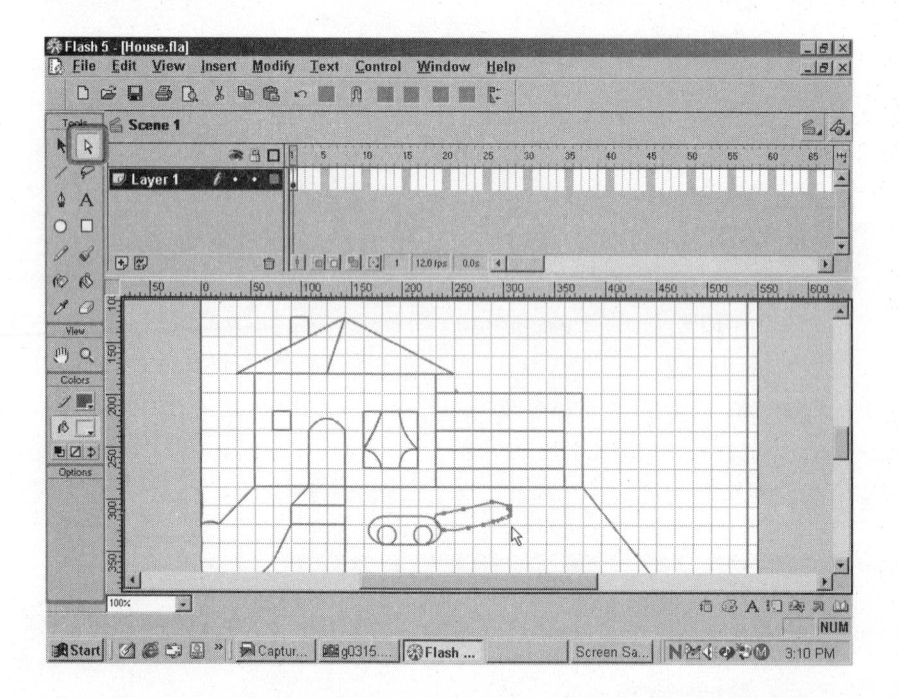

Tip

The difference between the Arrow tool and the Subselect tool is that the Subselect tool forms handles (points for manipulation) around the selected object, whereas the Arrow presents right angle or arc symbols to indicate the line type to be formed. The Subselect tool is comparable to Bezier or path tools found in many draw and paint programs.

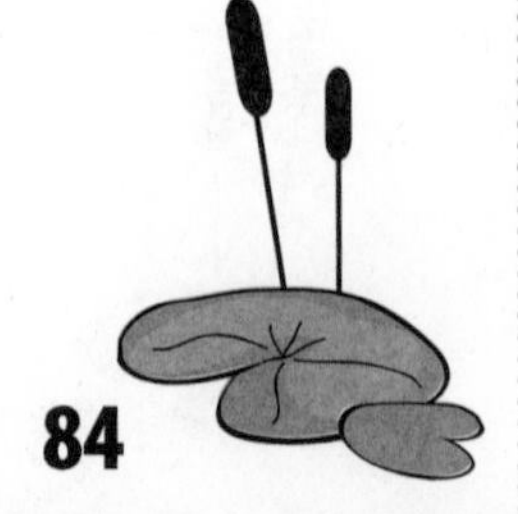

Using the Painting Tools

Working only with line drawings might be fine for drawing house plans, but it isn't as much fun as adding color and other enhancements to your movie. Line drawings have their place on the Web, but you wouldn't want to use them exclusively.

When you paint in Flash, you use the painting tools—the Brush tool, the **Ink Bottle tool**, the **Paint Bucket tool**—as well as the Eraser. The Brush and the Paint Bucket both use the fill color to paint, whereas the Ink Bottle tool uses line color. Let's use them to add some character to the house.

Filling in Areas of the House

The Paint Bucket is one of the most versatile tools. With it you can fill closed areas with color and even fill in gaps where the lines don't quite meet. You can use the colors in the palette, mix your own colors, and use **gradients** as fill as well. Let's start by filling:

1. Select the mower body and then select Modify ➢ Break Apart to break the mower group apart for further editing of its wheels and body.

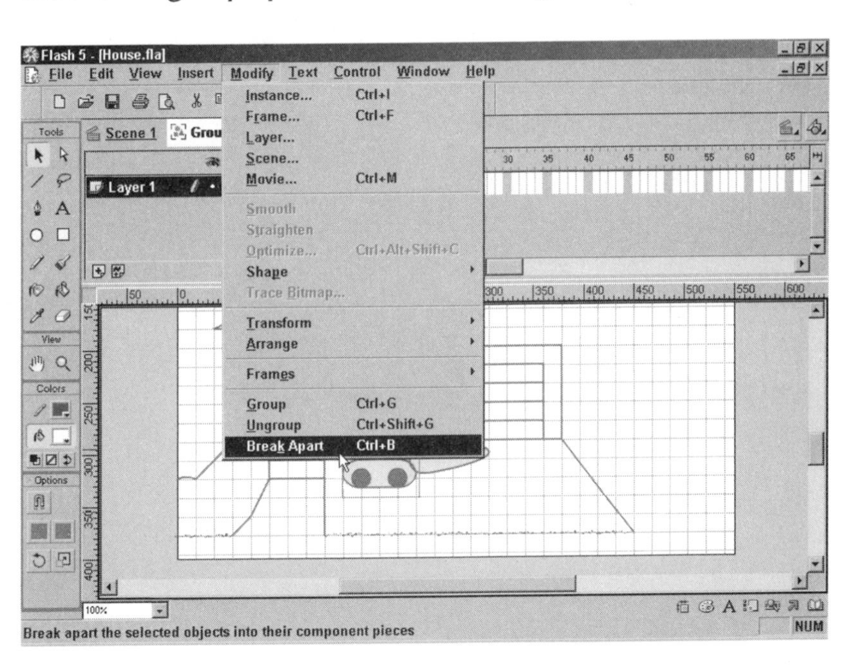

Ink Bottle tool

Use the Ink Bottle tool to modify the color and stroke of lines. You can change the width and style of a line as well as the color by selecting Window ➢ Panels ➢ Stroke while the Ink Bottle tool is selected.

Paint Bucket tool

Use the Paint Bucket tool to fill in closed areas. Lines must surround the areas. You can control the size of gaps that will be filled in by using the tool modifiers in the Options box. You can select from a range of options: from no gaps closed to large gaps closed.

gradient

Use gradients to combine different colors or shades in increasing or decreasing amounts so that colors fade in and out or are replaced by bands of other colors. In Flash, gradients are either linear or radial.

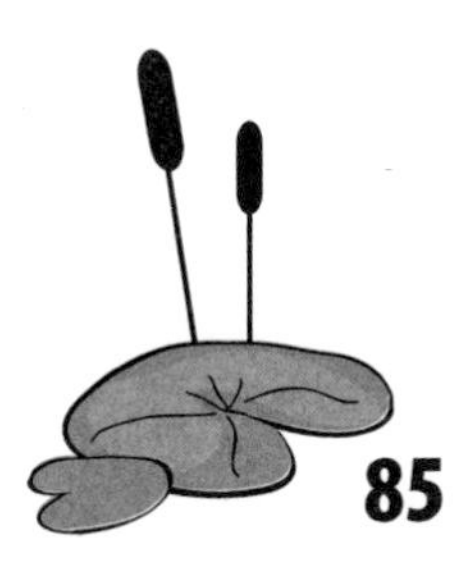

2. Select the Paint Bucket, select a blue-gray fill shade from the Colors box, and click inside each wheel. Change the blue to a bright yellow shade and click inside the mower body to color it a different color.

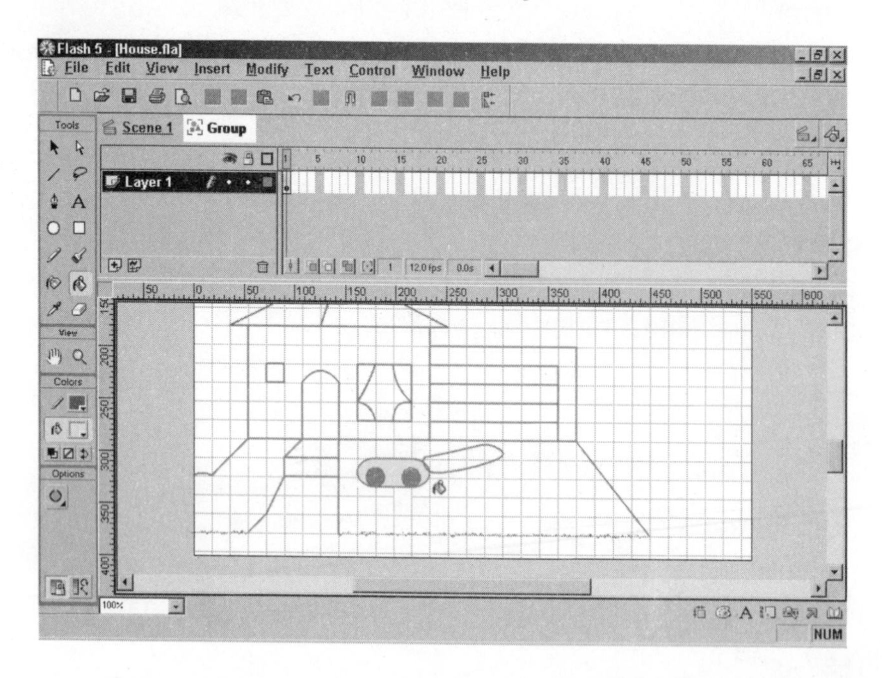

3. Now click inside the mower handle. Oops! That is a mistake. Select the fill inside the handle.

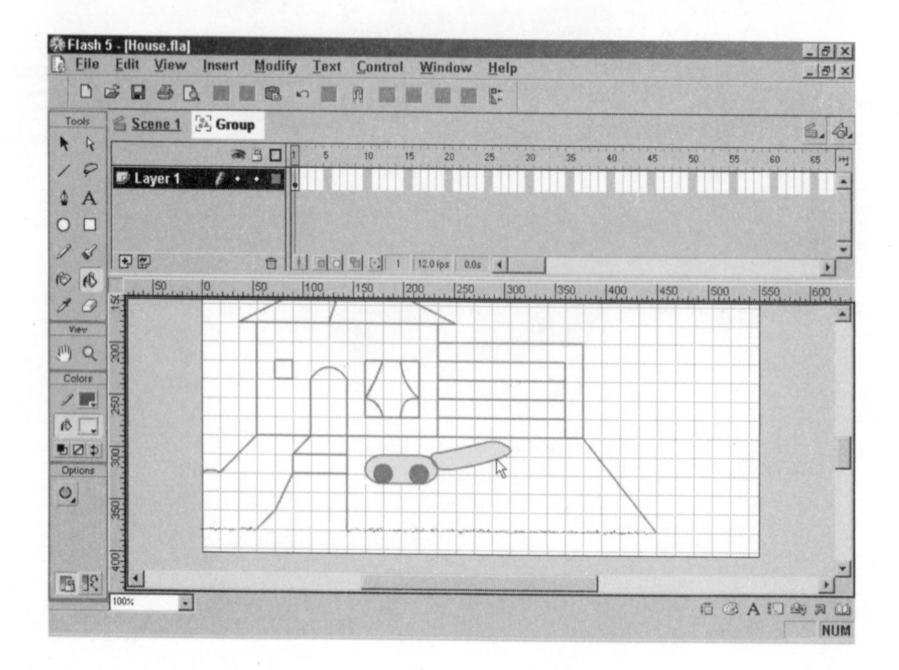

4. Select the Eraser tool. Click the Eraser Mode button in the Options box and choose Erase Selected Fills. Draw the Eraser over the yellow fill inside the handle to erase it.

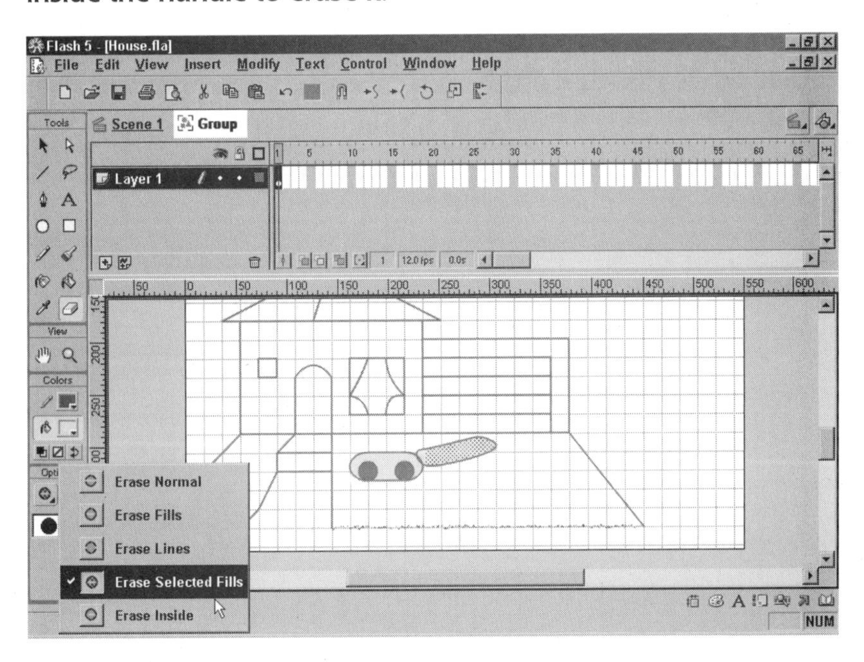

5. Select a green fill color from the Colors box and select the Paint Bucket. Click on the lawn area. Click inside the handle area as well. If you have enclosed the lawn area, it will fill with green grass. If not, the entire Stage will be painted. If that happens, just select Edit ➢ Undo.

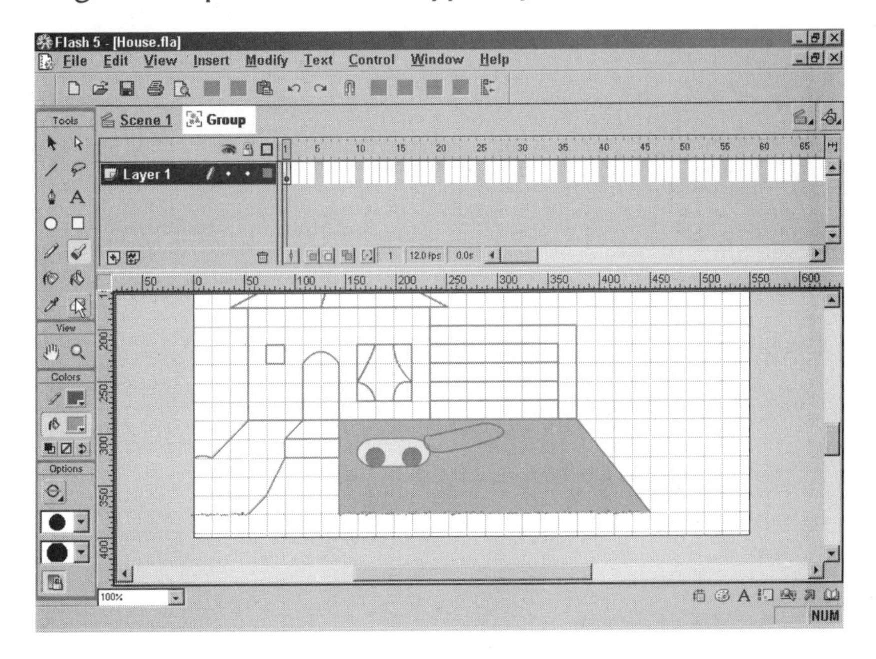

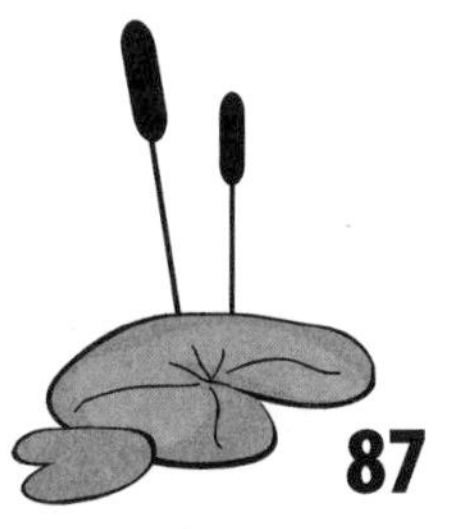

6. Using the Paint Bucket, click on the lawn to the left of the step. It doesn't work unless you connected all the lines bordering the lawn. You can try using the Paint Bucket Close Large Gaps mode to fill the left lawn area, but if the gap is too big, it won't work. You can select the Pencil tool and draw a vertical line to close the gap on the edge of the Stage and then use the Paint Bucket to fill it in.

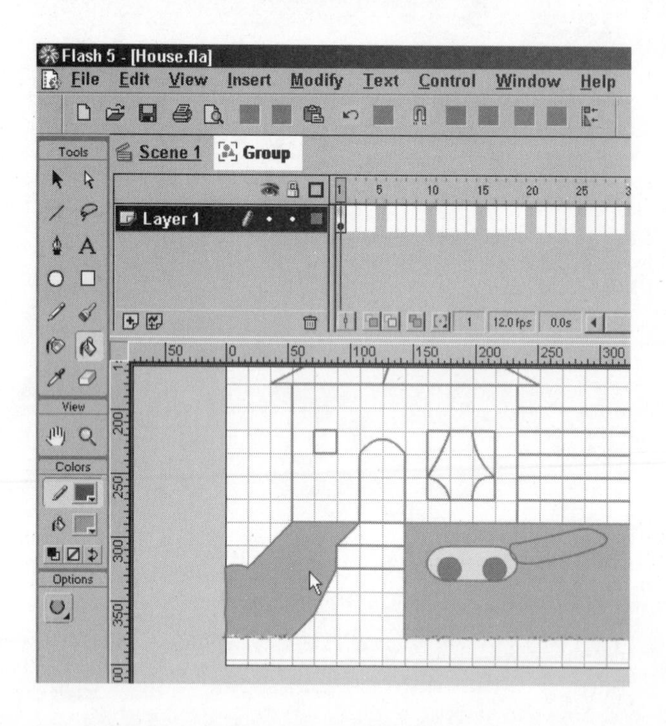

Brush tool

Use the Brush tool to paint areas with the fill color. You can change the shape and size of the brush stroke. Modify the Brush tool by selecting Window ➢ Panels ➢ Fill or by using the Brush tool options (at the bottom of the Toolbox).

Painting Areas with the Brush Tool

The **Brush tool** paints with fill color according to the brush size and shape. Let's try it:

1. Select the Eraser tool and the Erase Fills mode. Use the tool to erase the left lawn area just filled.
2. Select the Brush tool and use it to paint inside the lawn portion to the left of the front step. Do you find that more difficult than using the Paint Bucket tool? The Brush will overwrite lines rather than filling an area with color inside the lines. In the next step, you will learn how to correct that.

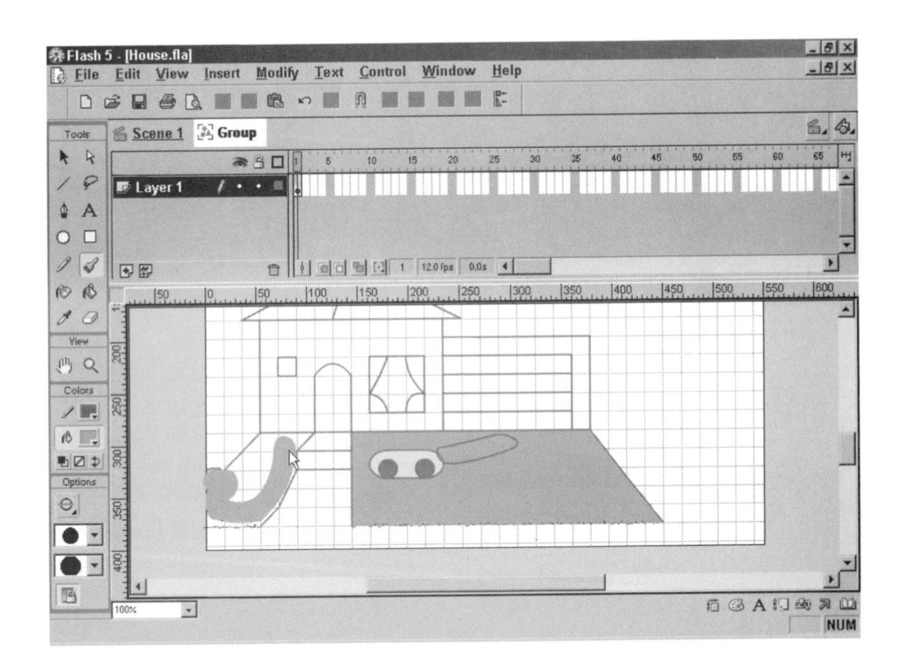

3. Select the Arrow tool and then double-click on the lawn. Select the Brush tool and check the brush size. From the drop-down menu, select a brush size and shape that are appropriate for the area you are painting. Click the Brush Mode button in the Options box. Select the Paint Inside mode and paint the left lawn.

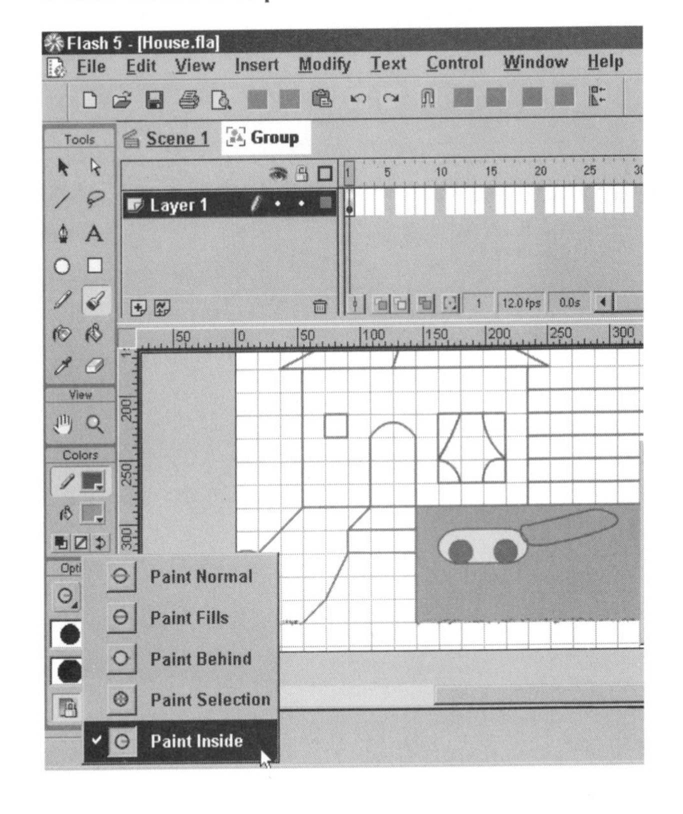

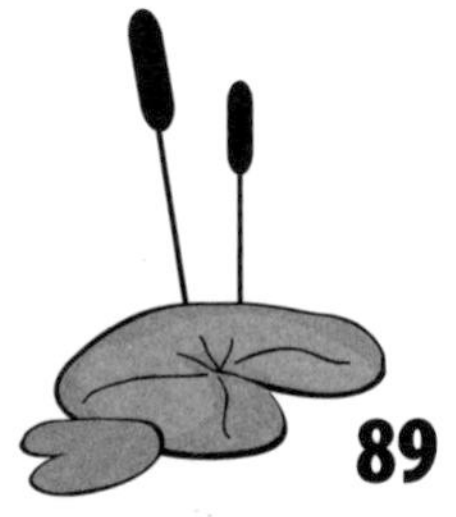

4. Paint the left lawn, covering the entire area. There is no need to try to stay inside the lines as long as you use the Paint Inside option.

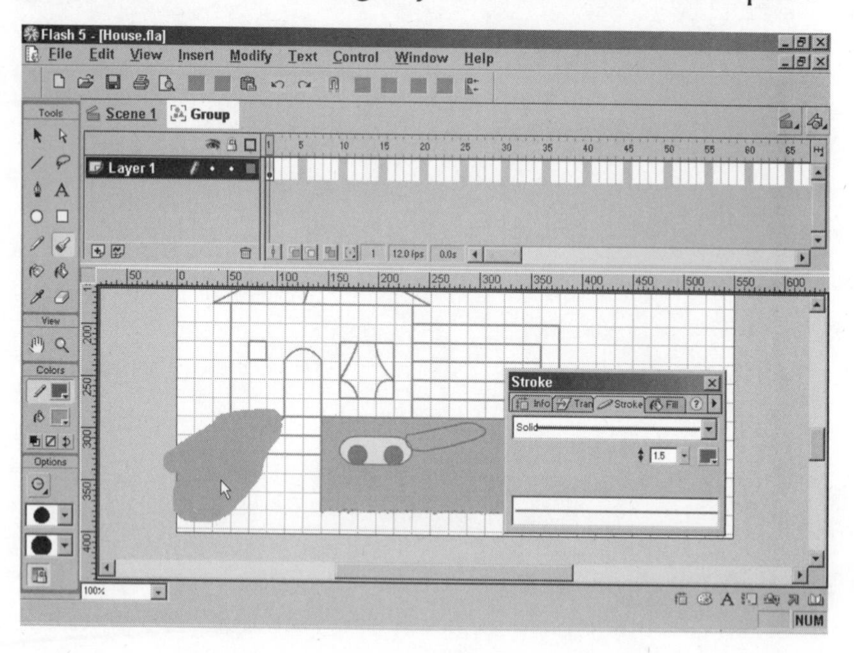

5. Select Edit ➢ Undo to remove the grass you just painted. Select the Brush tool again and the Paint Behind Paint mode. Now repaint the left lawn. How does that work? Select Edit ➢ Undo or the Undo icon from the Windows toolbar so you can remedy the situation. Select the Brush tool and the Paint Inside Paint mode and redo step 3.

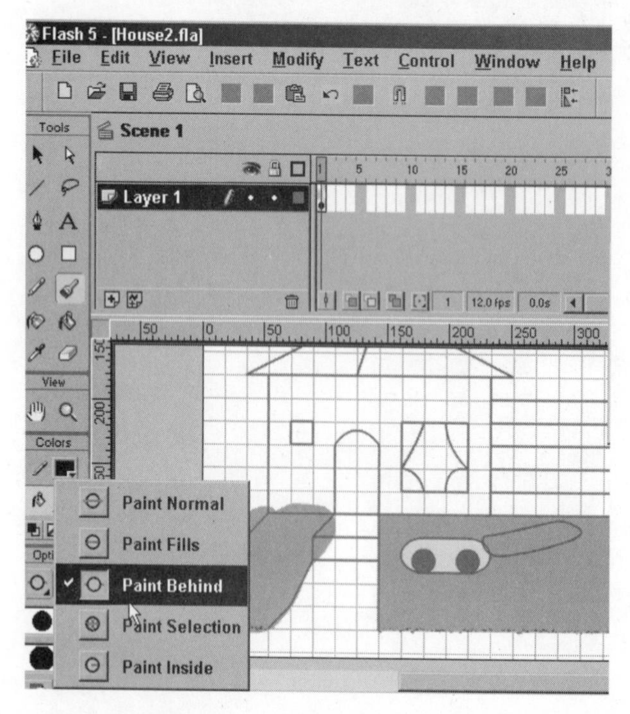

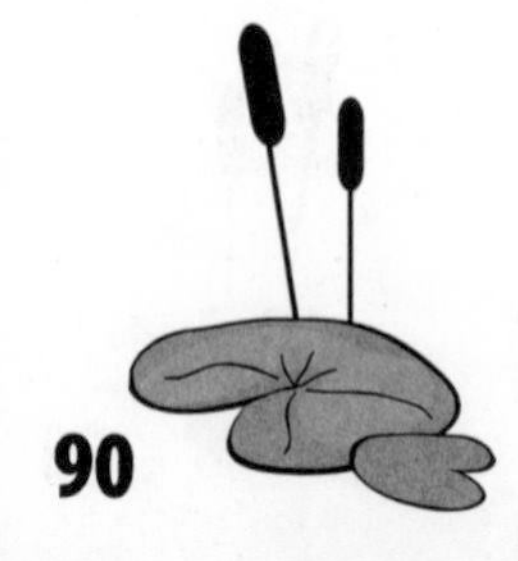

Note

Notice that while you are painting, the paint appears to float over the lines into the surrounding area, but it fits inside when you release the mouse button.

6. Now, select the painted area using the Arrow tool. Select the Brush tool and the Paint Selection Paint mode. Select a slightly different shade of green and paint over the area you just painted.

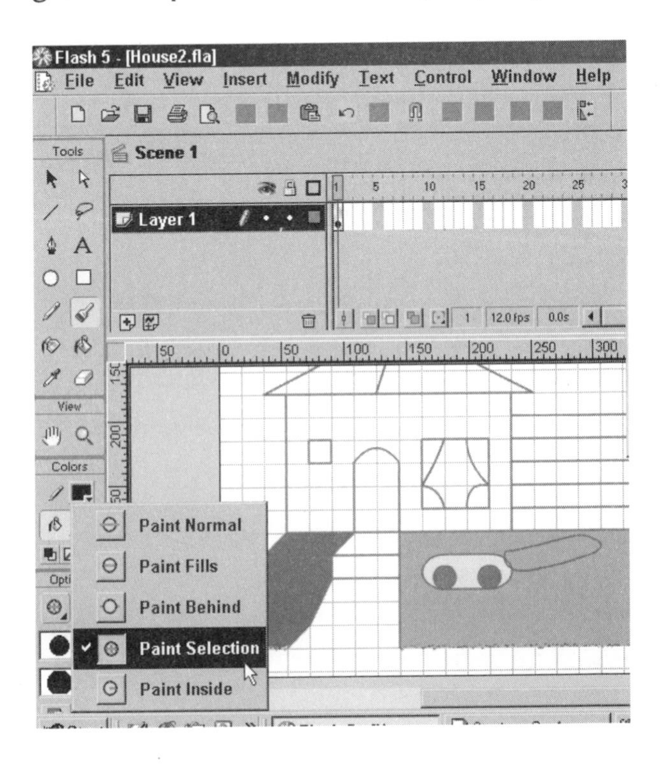

Creating a Sky with the Paint Bucket Tool

You can use the Paint Brush to color the sky, but the Paint Bucket tool will make the job easier:

1. The picture needs a sky. Select View ➢ Zoom Out to see the whole Stage. Pick a blue line color. Select the Pencil tool and then select the Straighten Lines mode from the Options box. Draw a line around the entire Stage, including a large area around the house connecting to each of the lines delineating the lawn areas.

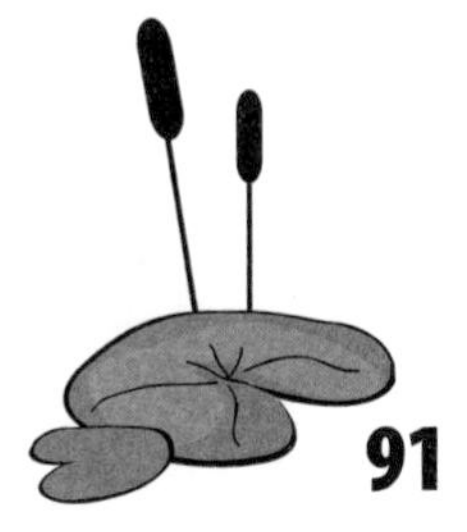

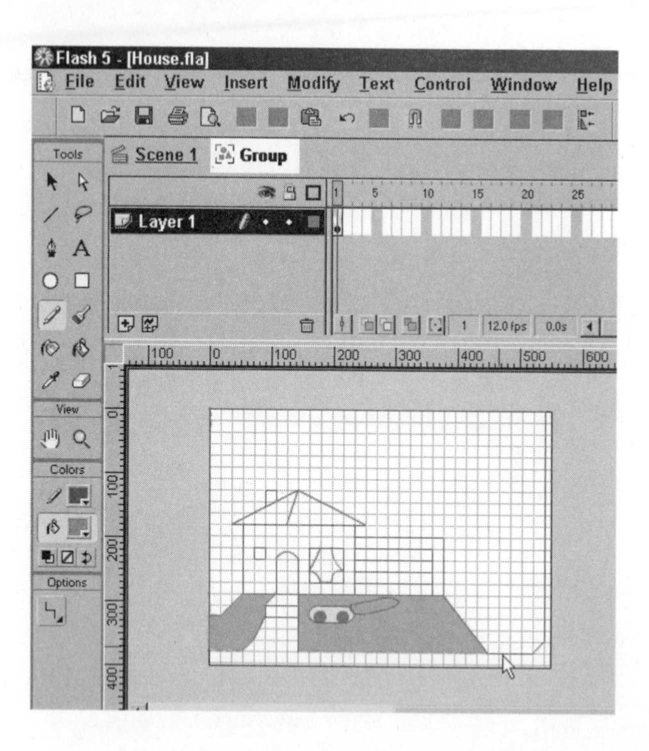

2. Select a light blue fill color for the sky. Select the Paint Bucket tool and click inside the sky area.

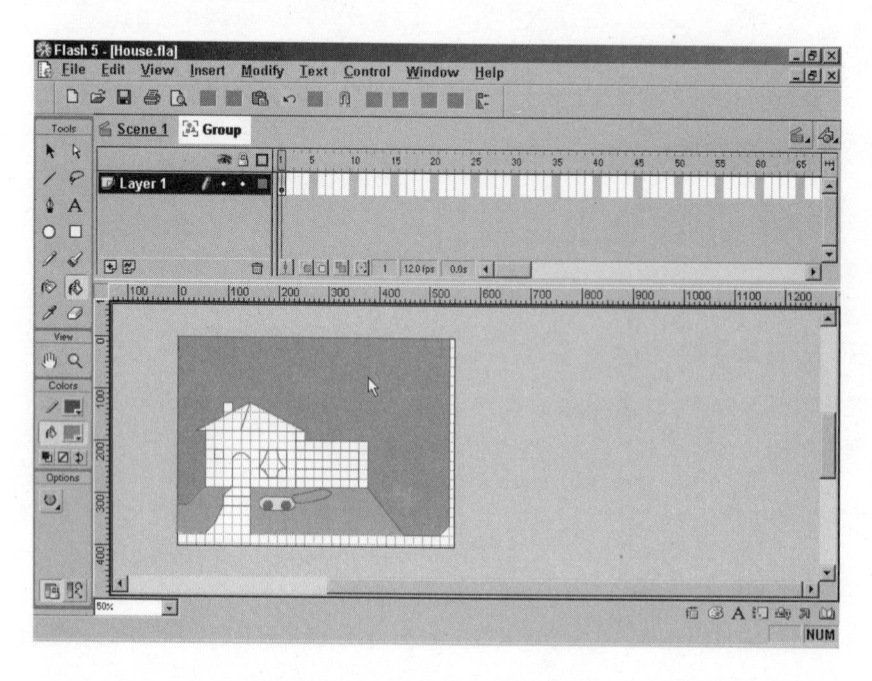

3. Make some clouds for your scene. Select a very light blue fill color from the Colors box. Use the Brush tool to paint clouds over the house.

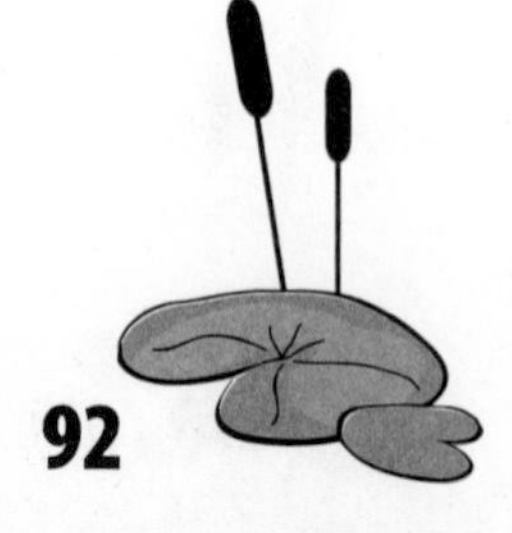

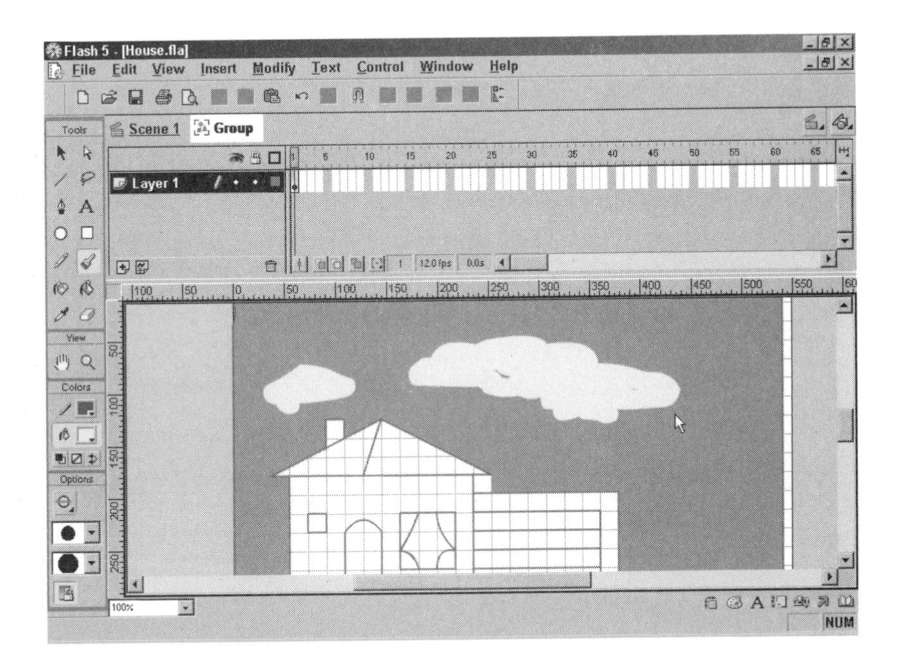

Painting Gradient Fills

Many times in Flash, as in other applications, there are several ways to do the same or similar tasks. Optionally, the sky can be done as a gradient. Gradients are important for depth perception because they give the impression of a three-dimensional object. Let's use the gradient.

Painting the Sky with Gradients

The gradient you view in the Fill Panel will be based on the gradient fill that was last selected via the Fill button in the Colors box. If none was selected, the black and white gradient will be used by default:

1. Select the sky by double-clicking it and then press the Delete key. Or, select the sky and use the Eraser and the Eraser mode Erase Selected Fills to erase the sky.

Tip

It is a good idea to save your file periodically and also occasionally use Save As to save the file under more than one name. That way, if your work is hopelessly ruined, you can revert to another file.

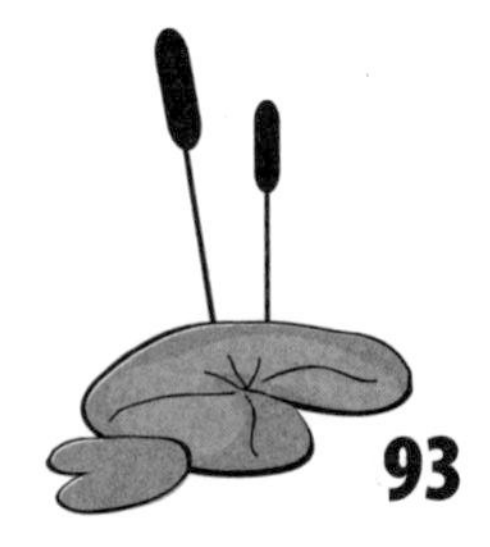

2. Select a blue fill shade, then select Window ➢ Panels ➢ Fill. Select Radial Gradient from the drop-down menu.

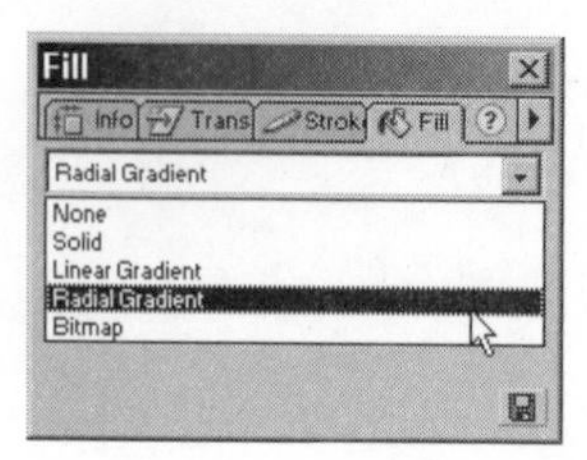

Tip

You can use either the Paint Bucket or the Brush tool to paint gradient fills.

Mixing a Gradient Fill

You can select a gradient by using the Fill button in the Colors box below the Toolbox.

Note

If you initially select a gradient from the Fill styles in the Fill Panel window, pointers will appear under the gradient slider bar. You must click on the pointers to make the Color Palette button appear.

1. Select a color from the Palette button on the right side of the Fill Panel window. This will set the basis for the gradient. Move the pointers displayed below the slider bar to change the color mix until you are satisfied with the gradient.

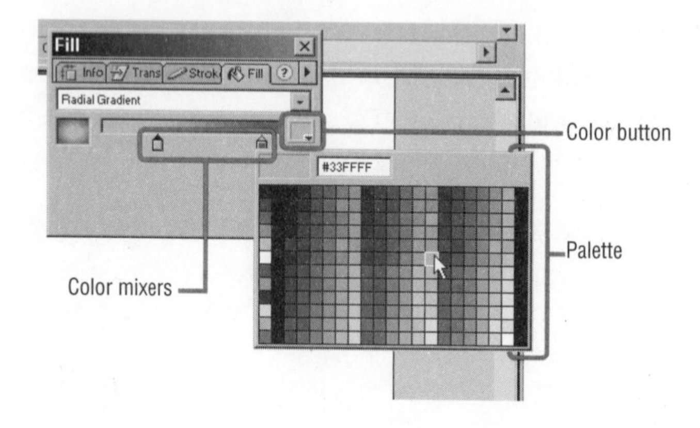

2. Select a gradient by using the Fill button in the Colors box. A linear gradient will work for this as well as a radial one. Select Window ➢ Panels ➢ Fill.
3. Move the color mixer tabs along the gradient box until you like the result.
4. Click the Save button to save the color. When you open the Fill palette, you will see the new gradient you created.

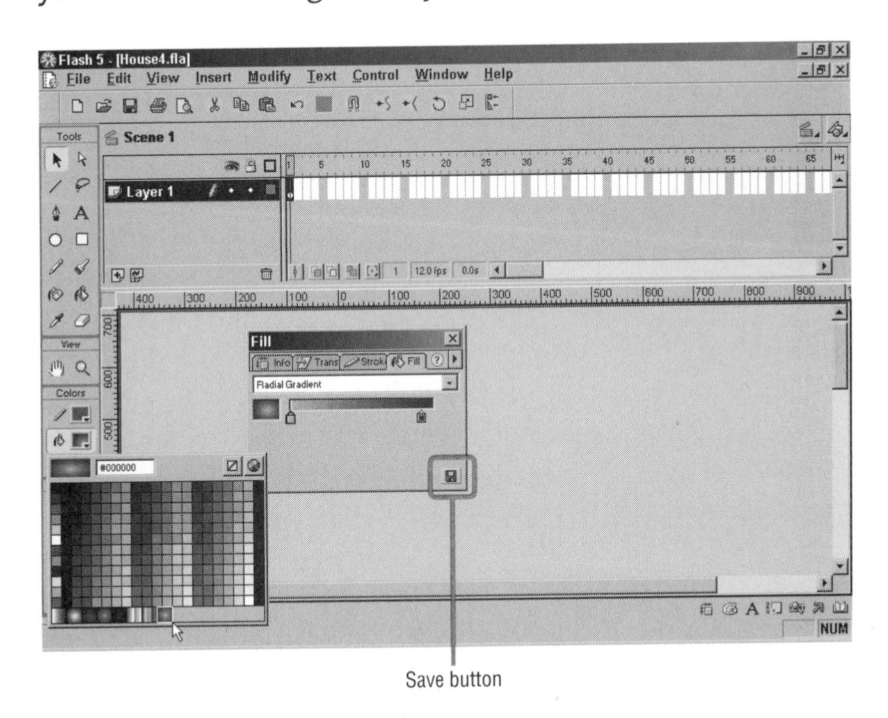

Save button

Applying the Gradient Fill to the Sky

Using a gradient fill for the sky will offer a depth perspective not provided by a solid fill color:

1. Try the new gradient on a blank Stage by selecting File ➢ New or by clicking the New File icon on the toolbar. Use the Window menu to switch back to the house drawing when you're done trying out the gradient.

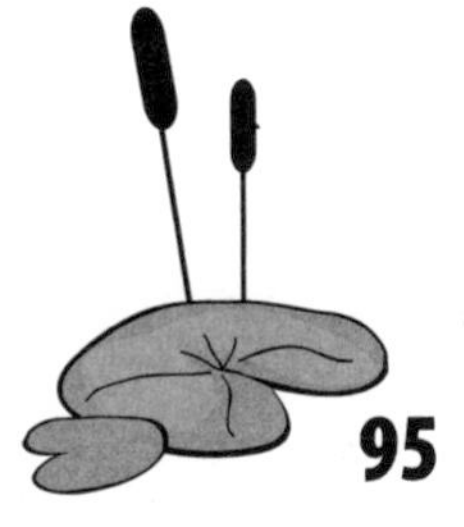

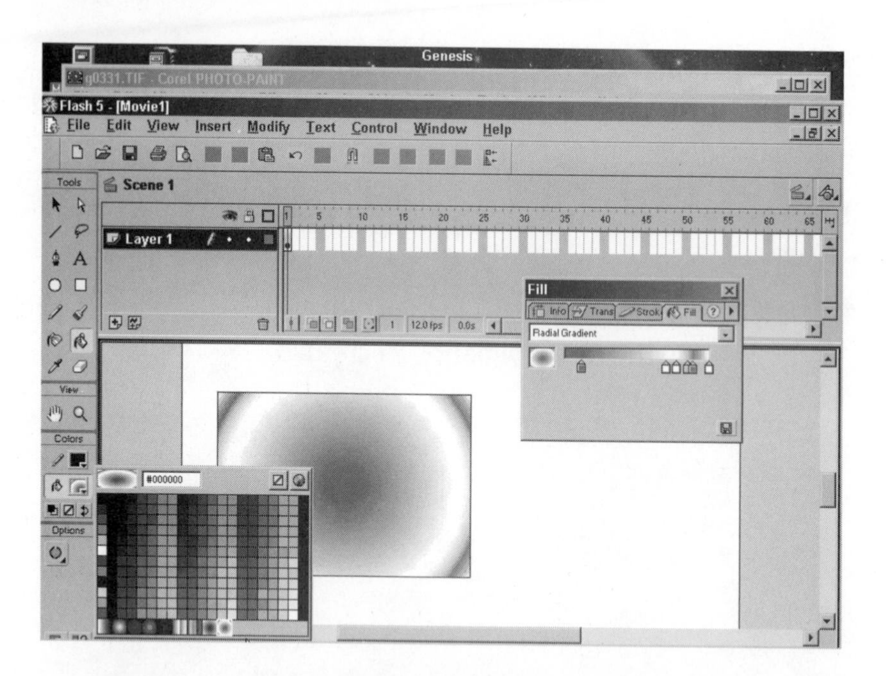

2. Finally, with the new gradient selected as the fill color, select the Paint Bucket tool and click inside the sky area. You also can use the Brush tool to paint the gradient. Because you have replaced the original sky with a gradient, the clouds no longer appear. Now you can embellish the sky with clouds if you wish.

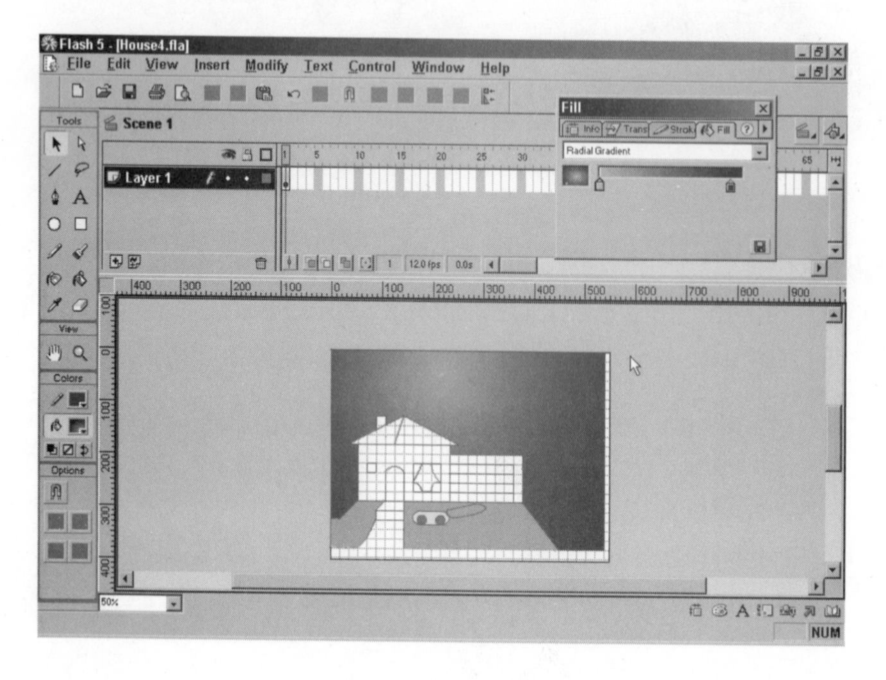

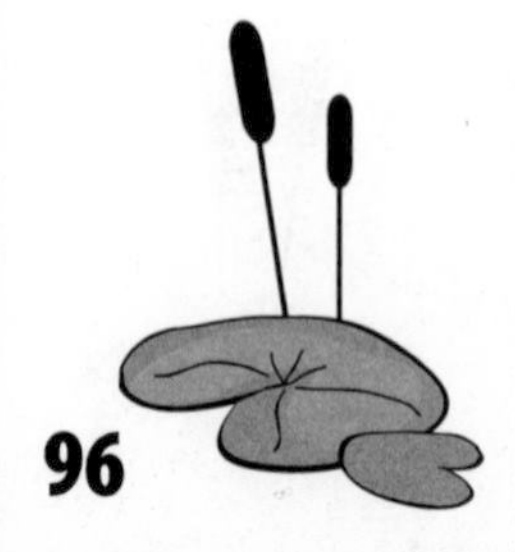

3. Complete your house by filling in the remaining areas. You can use the Brush tool to paint inside areas or use the Paint Bucket tool to fill in each section. Use contrasting shades of the same color for shaded areas for a three-dimensional look. Remember to save your work frequently (File ➢ Save or click the disk icon on the toolbar).

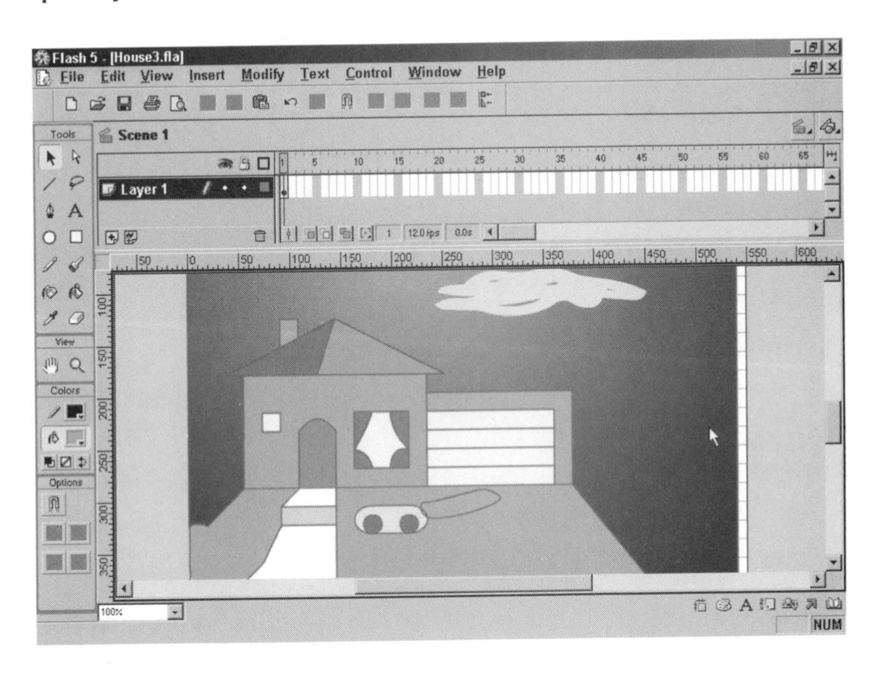

Redefining the Lines of the House with the Ink Bottle

The Ink Bottle tool is used to define or redefine lines. You can select the Ink Bottle tool and then select the Stroke attributes you want to use to change the lines in your house. Let's change them:

1. Select the Ink Bottle tool. Select Window ➢ Panels ➢ Stroke. Click the Color button to select a dark brown. Use the Ink Bottle tool to darken the rooflines of the house.
2. You can select different line styles to get different effects. Select the wavy broken line and change the line width to 2 points to modify the roofline.

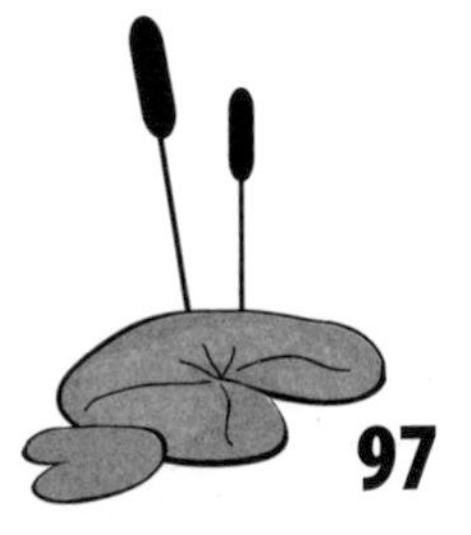

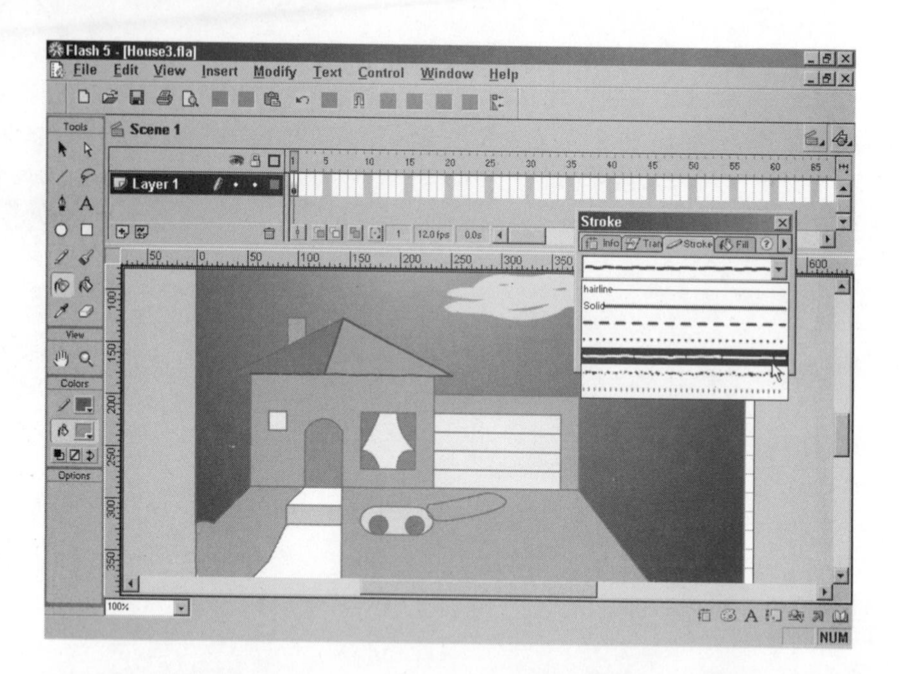

3. Select the dotted line, then use the Ink Bottle tool to change the line between the house and the lawn. This gives it the appearance of a plant border.

4. Continue using the Ink Bottle tool to enhance the house. It is easy to get carried away and draw something inappropriate, but remember to save and use the Undo feature as needed.

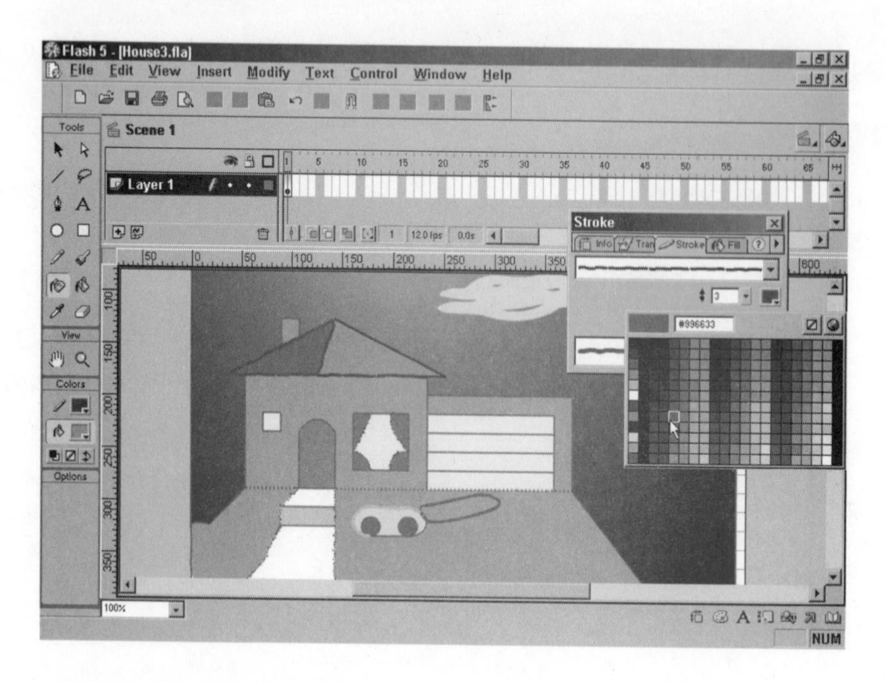

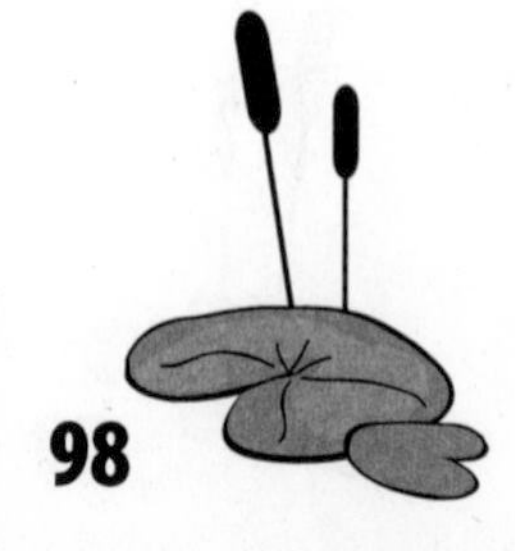

Using the Lasso to Create a Driveway

It's time to add a driveway to the house. In fact, you can most likely now figure out more than one way to do it. There is at least one way you have not yet explored. Let's use the Lasso tool:

1. Open your house movie file and select the Lasso tool.
2. Click the Polygon modifier in the Options box below the Toolbox and use it to draw a line from the left side of the garage to the street (beyond the sidewalk); when you get to the street, click the mouse button. Continue across the driveway to the area in line with the garage and click when you get to the other side. Move along the yard to the right side of the garage and double-click to end the drawing.

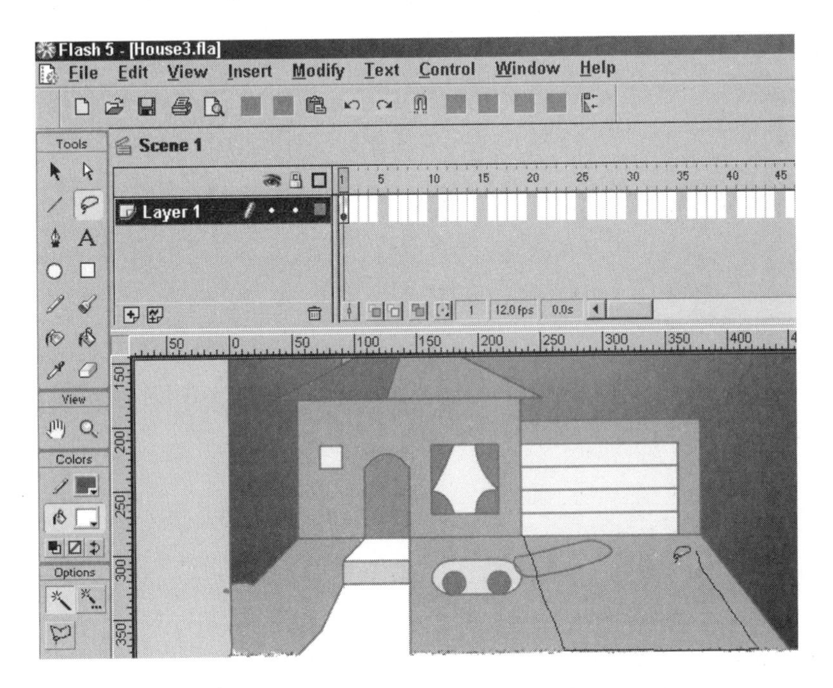

3. After the double-click, you should have a selection area showing in the driveway area.

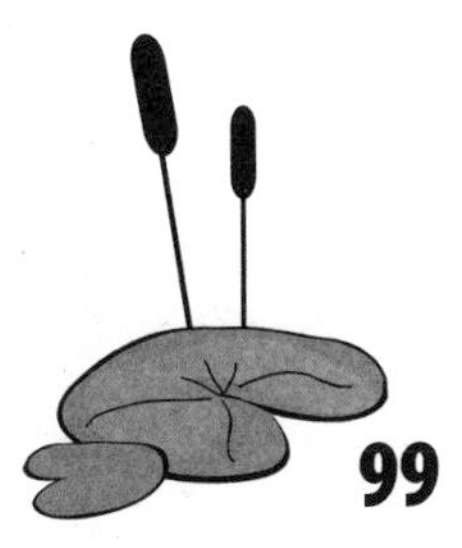

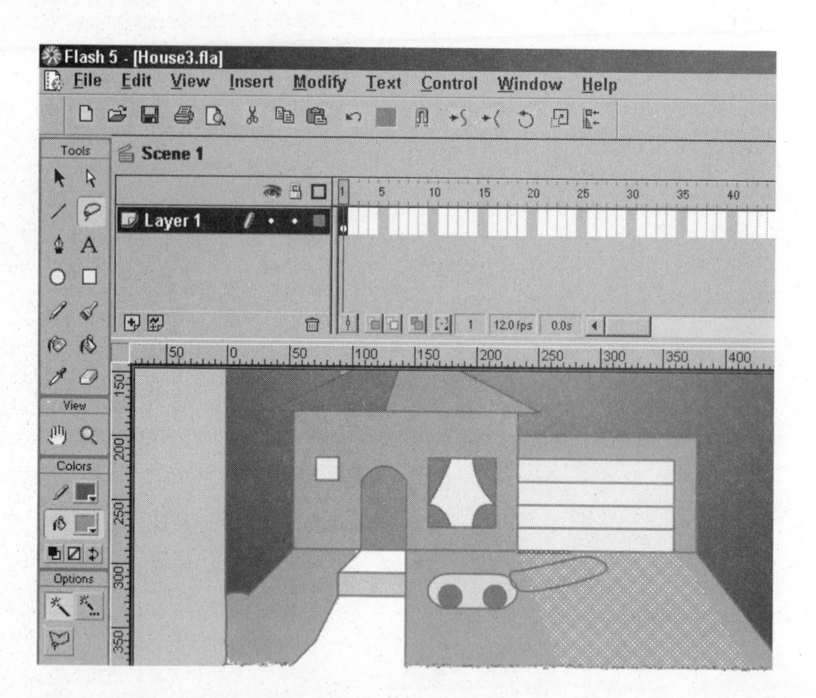

4. Select a grayish fill color by using the Fill button in the Colors box. Once selected, the color fills in the selection area.

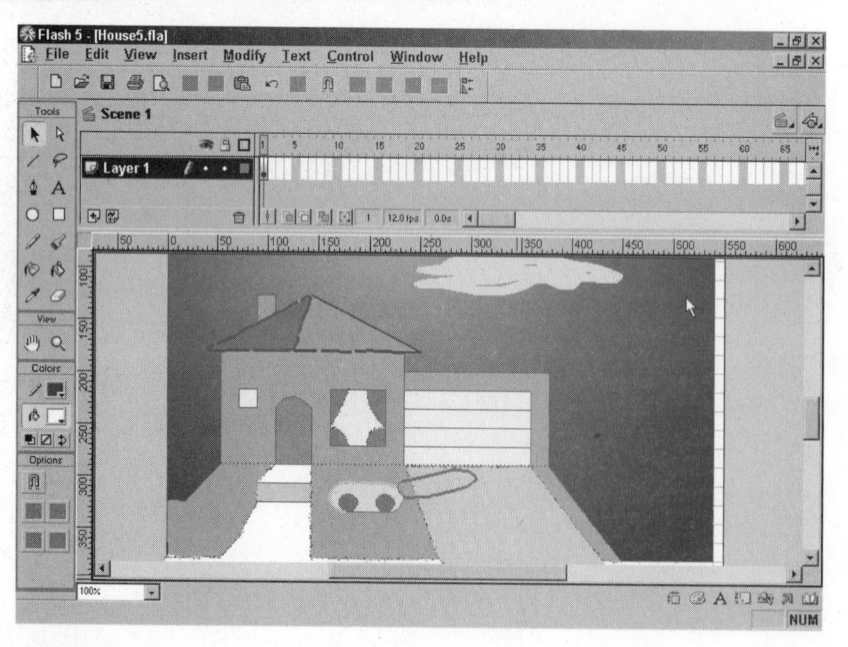

5. You can continue to enhance your picture by using the Ink Bottle to create a jagged line along the driveway to simulate grass if you wish.

Now that you have become proficient at drawing and painting your house, you are ready to move on to learning about and using symbols and instances.

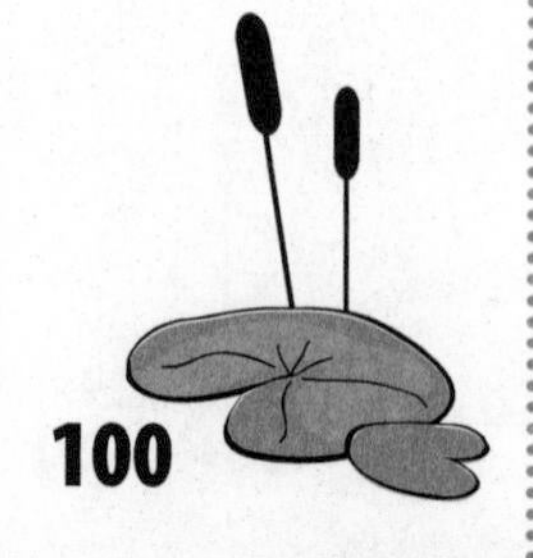

Chapter 4

Creating and Using Symbols

One of the most important features in Flash is that it gives you the ability to create a prototype you can use, change, and reuse. This prototype is called a symbol. Flash lets you create symbols, or reusable objects, and save them in a library for use in your movie. Like the automated animation, this is one of Flash's most powerful features. For example, you might convert a drawing of a circle to a symbol. You can then make copies of the symbol and thus reuse it. You can also modify these copies, or instances, of symbols. To make the best use of symbols, some planning is in order.

- Developing a Plan for Your Movie
- Working with Symbols
- Recognizing Instances

Developing a Plan for Your Movie

So far, you have been practicing and developing your skills with Flash. Learning how to develop a plan for your movies is just as important as learning how to use the tools. When you're creating a movie for a Web site, a little planning will go a long way.

Initial planning will save time in the long run because reworking a movie over and over takes a lot more time than getting it right the first time. With that in mind, let's create a scenario, design a menu, and plan some functions.

Creating a Scenario

plan
Use a plan to organize a set of tasks or functions. In this context, it refers to a scenario for a movie.

A **plan** does not have to be lengthy or complicated. You need to have a plan for what you intend to accomplish in terms of the general goals and specific functions of the movie. For example, you might design a menu around a home page, a products page, and a contact page. Thus, you have an outline of the features your project will include. Your menu will then include links to those pages.

Designing a Menu

menu
Use a menu as a set of options from which to choose. Most Windows and Macintosh applications provide a bar across the top of the screen with available menu options. Some menus drop down a list of options, some pop up, whereas others simply provide a text statement of the option offered.

A **menu** is a feature that every Web site has in some form or another. The menu consists of a set of options from which users can select. Menus can range from those displaying simple lines of text to those presenting any kind of fancy animation you can imagine, and some you can't imagine.

Note

The structure and design of a menu really depends upon the overall functions of the entire project.

Once you know what the functions of your site will be, you should design the menu around them. An example menu for the site we're creating would include Home, About Us, Products, and Contact. A simpler example would be Home, Services, and Feedback.

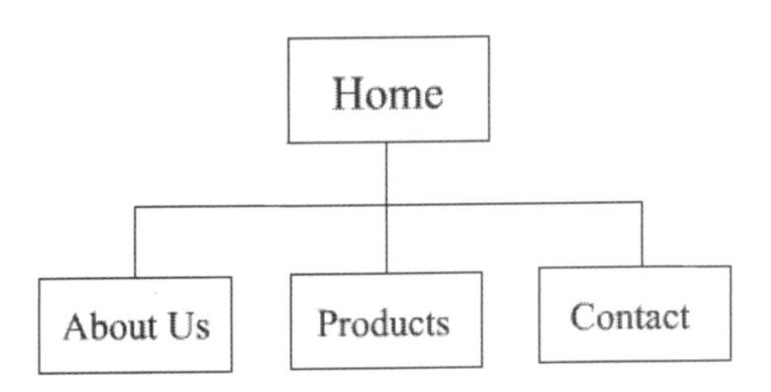

Viewing Menus on the Web

You can get a feel for the many types of menus on the Web by surfing a little. The next three illustrations each depict a slightly different treatment:

1. The first shows the primary menu as a button menu on the left side of the page.

2. The second site displays the primary menu across the top of the page.

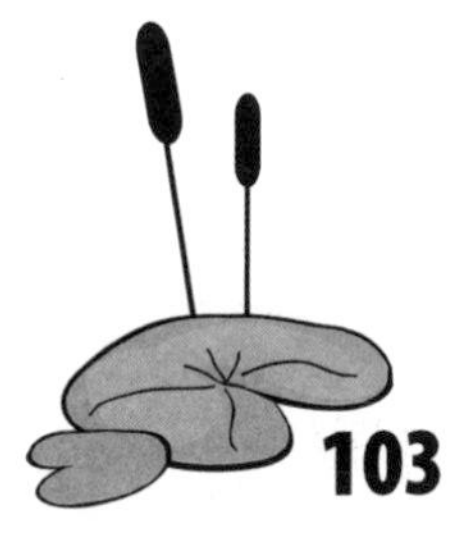

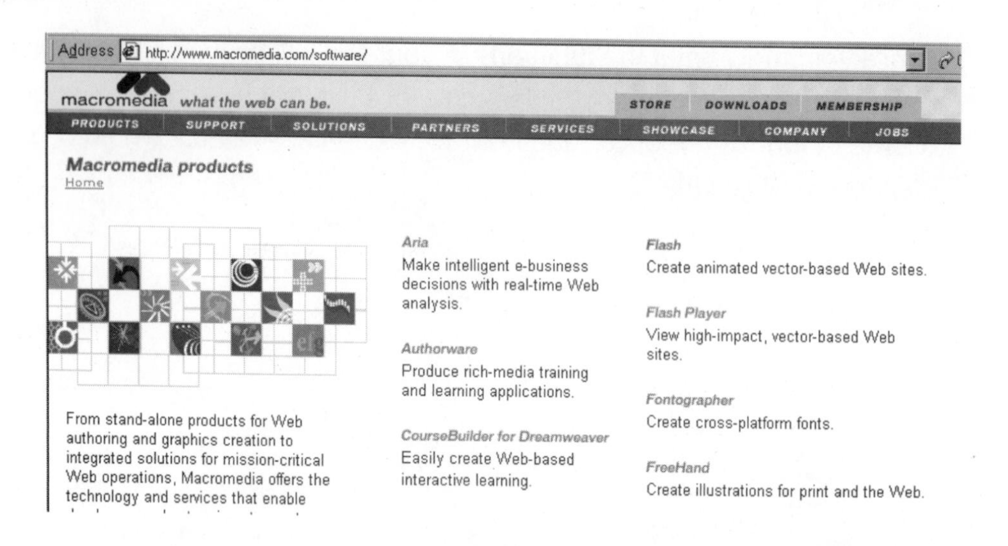

3. Most Web sites have more than one menu. On some sites, one menu is displayed along the left side of the page and another on the top or the bottom of the page. Sometimes, as with the Sybex site, menu options are just plain text.

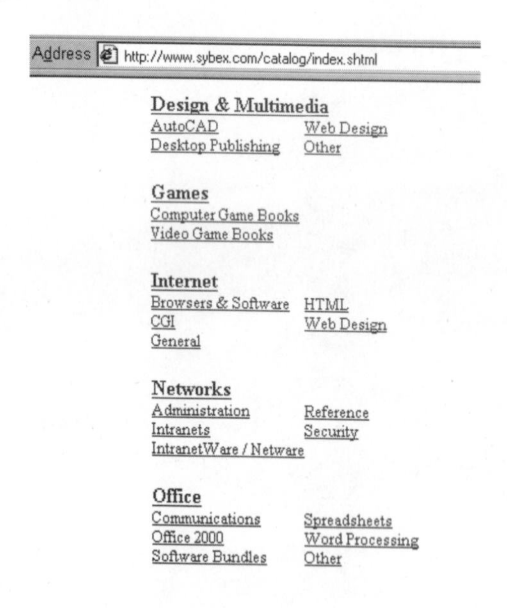

Planning Functions for Menu Design

The functions for your menus will be determined by the nature of the site. For example, if you are designing a stock market reporting site, your goals will be

different than they would be for an art and cultural center site. However, the menus on most sites share one goal: facilitating navigation.

Tip

Menus should be easy to find and options should be easy to understand.

Another important feature of menus is to carry out the theme of the Web site. A guitar manufacturer might tailor his menus to evoke a pop music mood.

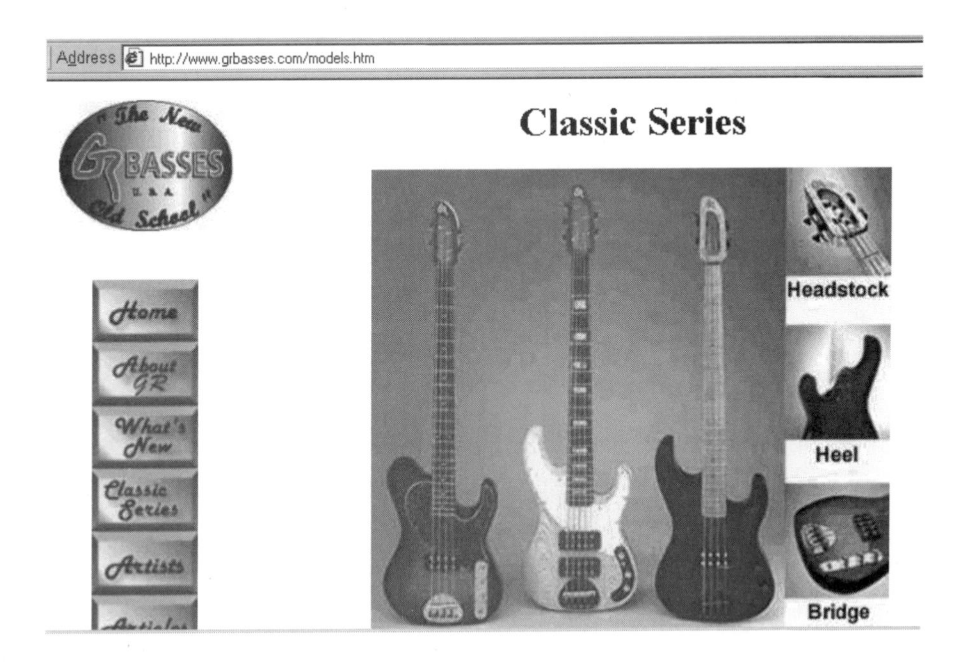

symbol

Symbols are reusable objects that are stored in the Library and can be dragged onto the Stage to be further modified. Converting objects to symbols reduces the size of the SWF file and conserves system resources (memory and, thus, download time).

Working with Symbols

When you convert an object to a symbol, you must define the properties' behavior as Movie Clip, Button, or Graphic. Of course, this determination depends upon what you have in mind for the symbol. If you are using the symbol as a prop in the scenery, you should select Graphic as the behavior. If you intend to use the symbol as a menu button, you should select Button as the behavior.

Creating a **symbol** is as easy as selecting an object and then selecting Insert ➢ Convert to Symbol.

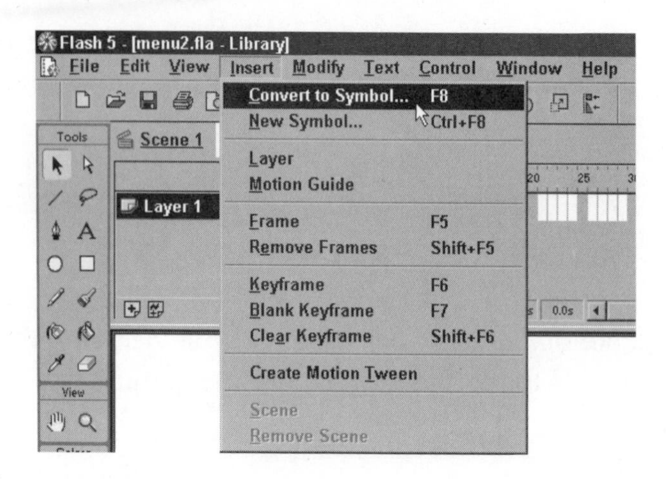

Using Graphic Symbols

You are going to design a tubelike cylinder with menu option buttons. The menu is for a sort of Art Deco style designer Web site. You must create a three-dimensional effect for the cylindrical tube. This movie can be found on the CD (`menu2.fla`). To design the tube, follow these steps:

1. Select the Rectangle tool, and then select the Round Rectangle Radius modifier from the Options box. Enter 10 points for the Corner Radius setting. Use File ➢ Save As to save your movie as Menu2.

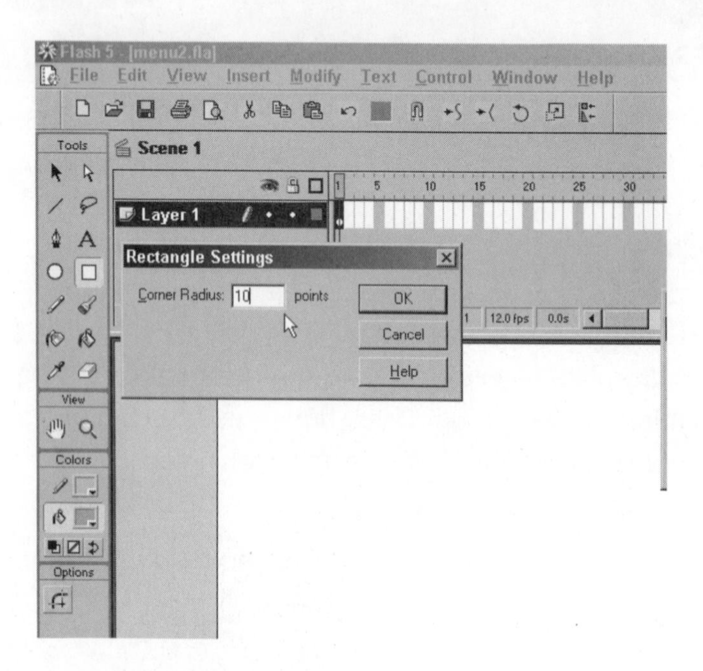

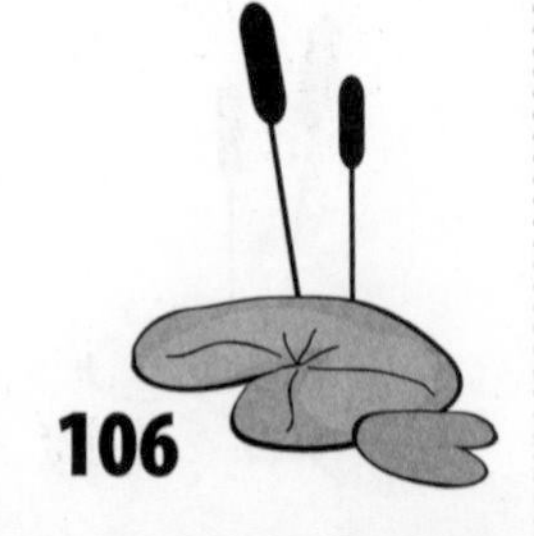

2. Select Window ➢ Panels ➢ Fill. Select Radial Gradient from the Fill Panel drop-down. Select the blue radial fill by using the Fill button in the Colors box. The fill color will appear in the Fill Panel.

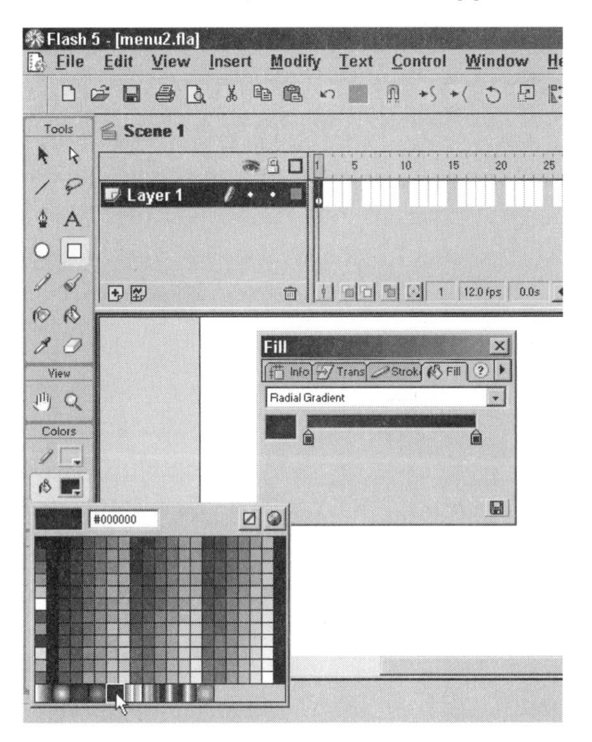

3. Select the blue marker under the gradient bar in the Fill Panel and then click the Color button on the right side of the Fill Panel. Choose a more muted dark blue from the palette pop-up window.

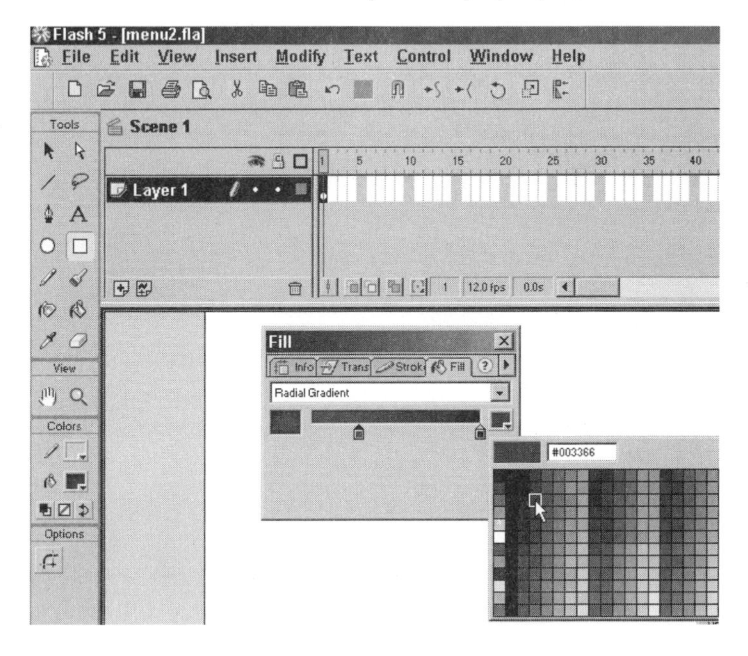

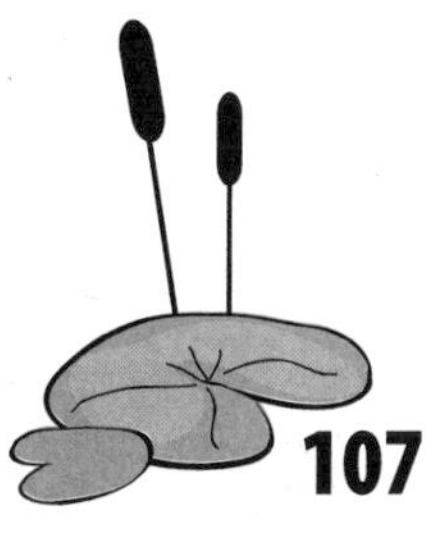

4. Now select Linear Gradient from the Fill Panel drop-down. Select the black pointer and click the Color button. Select light blue from the palette pop-up window. Now the light blue will replace the black in the original gradient. The gradient will change. The view button on the left side of the window shows a thumbnail of the gradient.

5. When you need to add an additional color to a gradient, you can force a new pointer to appear just by clicking in the gray area just under the gradient slider bar. Do not click on the existing pointers or in the slider bar itself.

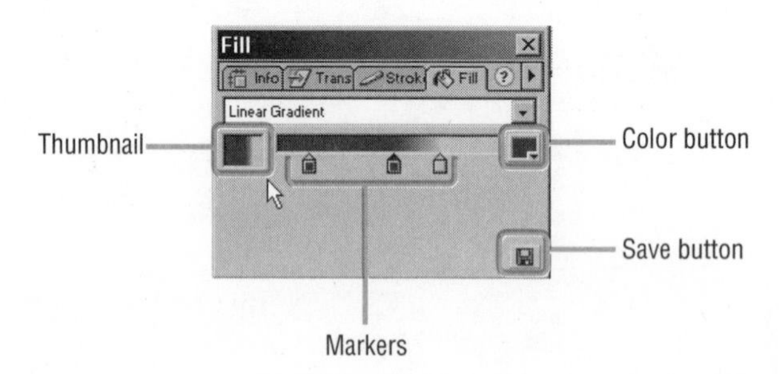

6. Slide the pointers back and forth along the gradient to produce a dark blue gradient with a smaller light blue middle area. The idea is to create a gradient that will make a rectangle look cylindrical.

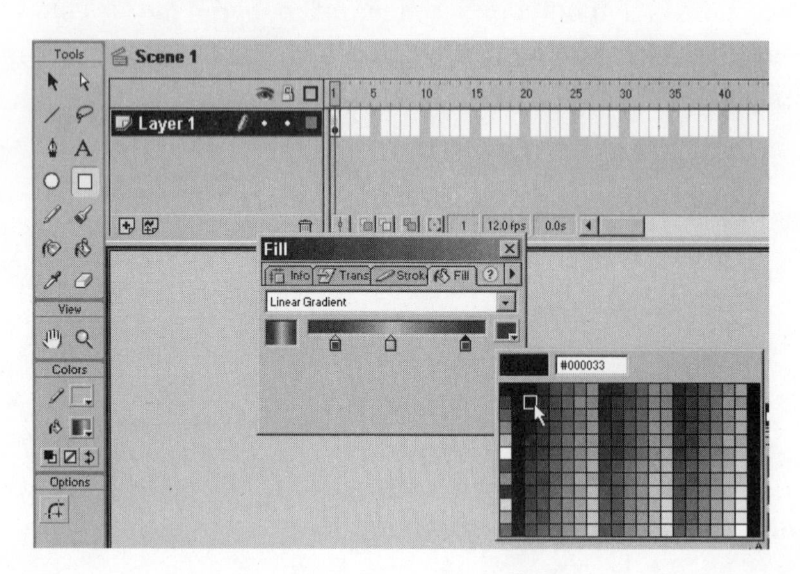

7. Select the Save button on the Fill Panel and then click the Fill button in the Colors box under the Toolbox to see the new fill you created. Use File ➢ Save to save your work.

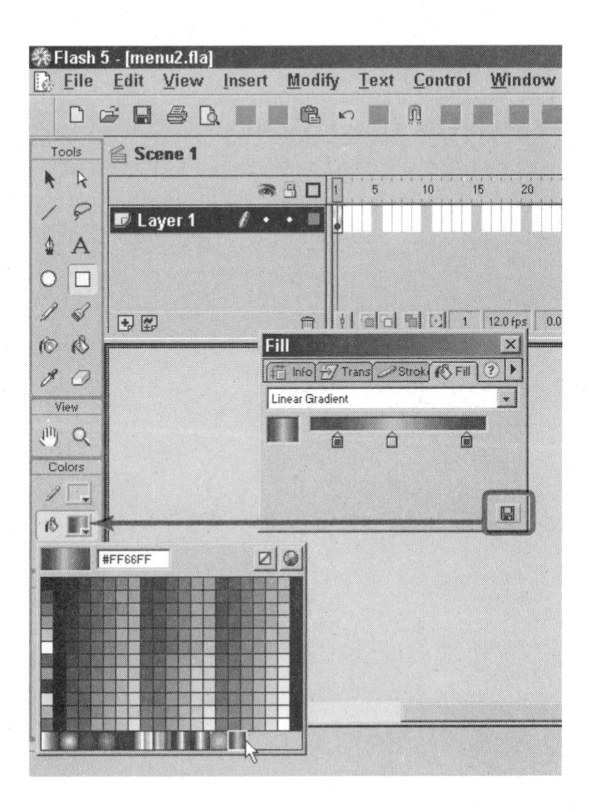

8. Select the Rectangle tool and draw a vertical rectangle on the Stage. The fill you just created and saved will be used to fill the rectangle.

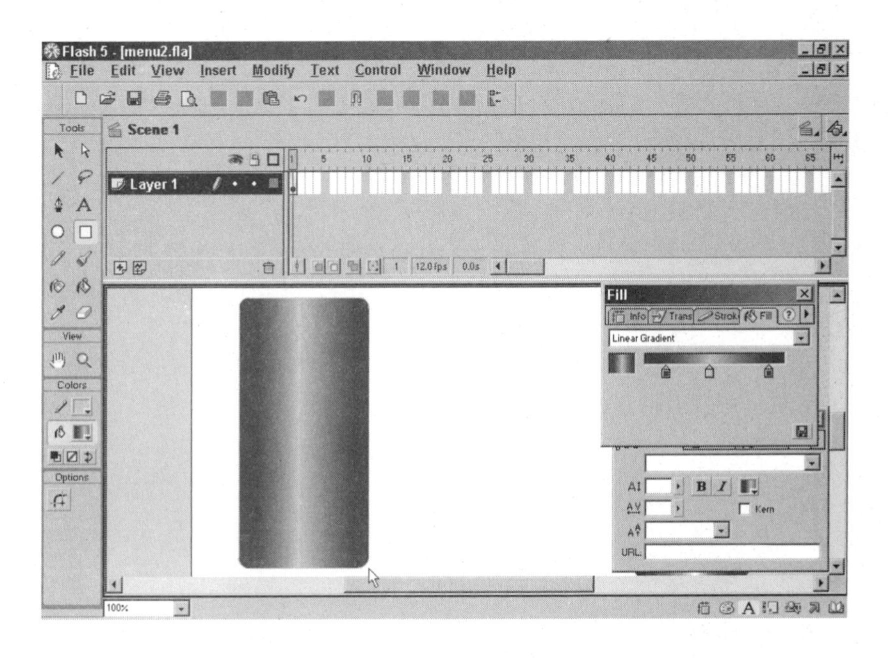

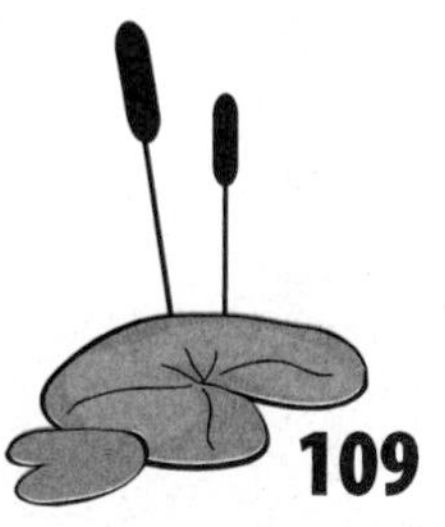

9. Once you are satisfied with the rectangle, you can create a symbol. Select the object you just drew and select Insert ➢ Convert to Symbol. Name the object "tube." Now tube will appear in the Library window. To see it, select Window ➢ Library.

Note

Once you convert the cylindrical rectangle to a symbol, it will be available to be reused and modified without having to re-create it. You can change the properties and effects of a symbol that will be used in animation.

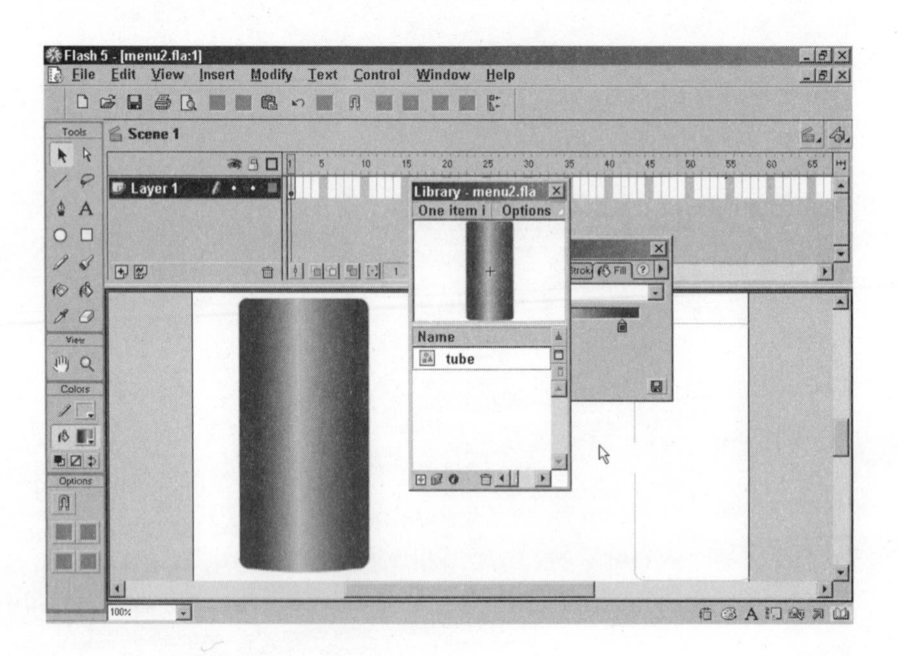

Creating and Using Buttons

button

A button is an object that contains a behavior specific to carrying out some action or event when activated.

Now, it's time to create some really cool buttons. The menu buttons should look as if they are floating on the cylinder, creating the impression of a tube with labels. You'll start by creating a new gradient, which you learned how to do in Chapter 3:

1. Create a new gradient for the **button**. Different tones of gold would contrast with the blue. Select Radial Gradient from the Fill Panel. Click the pointers below the gradient slider, selecting new colors from the palette until you have a gradient you like. The center should be lighter than the outer ring. Save the gradient and then select it from the color palette.

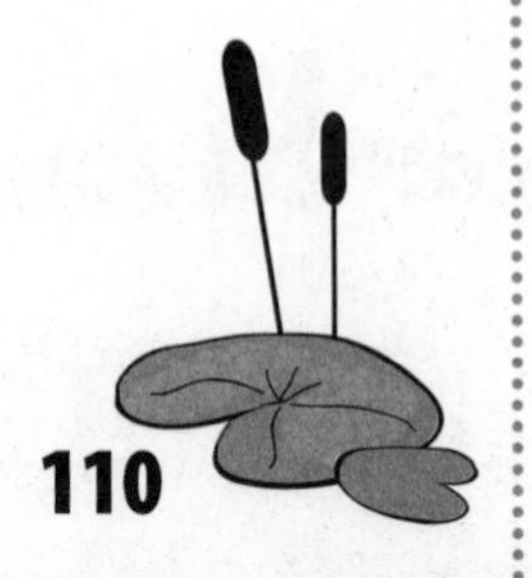

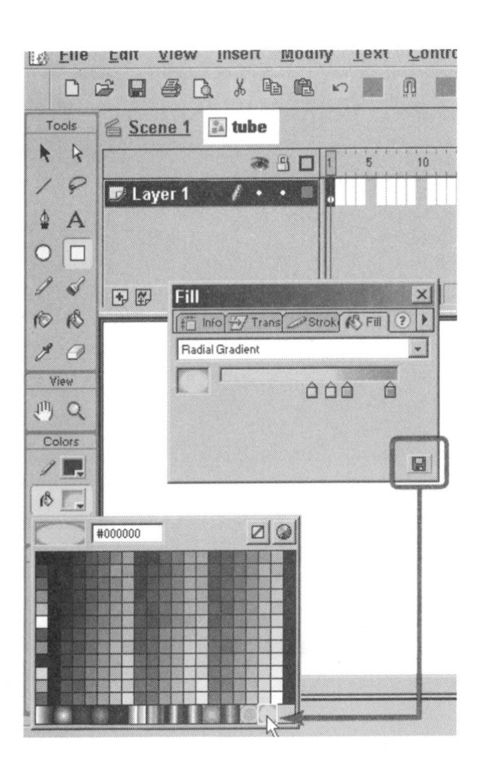

2. Draw a rectangular button with the Rectangle tool. Leave the setting for the round Rectangle Radius modifier at 10 points. The button should be sized to fit within the width of the cylinder and also small enough so that at least four buttons can be placed vertically. However, do not draw the button on the blue cylinder but, rather, on the Stage adjacent to the cylinder.

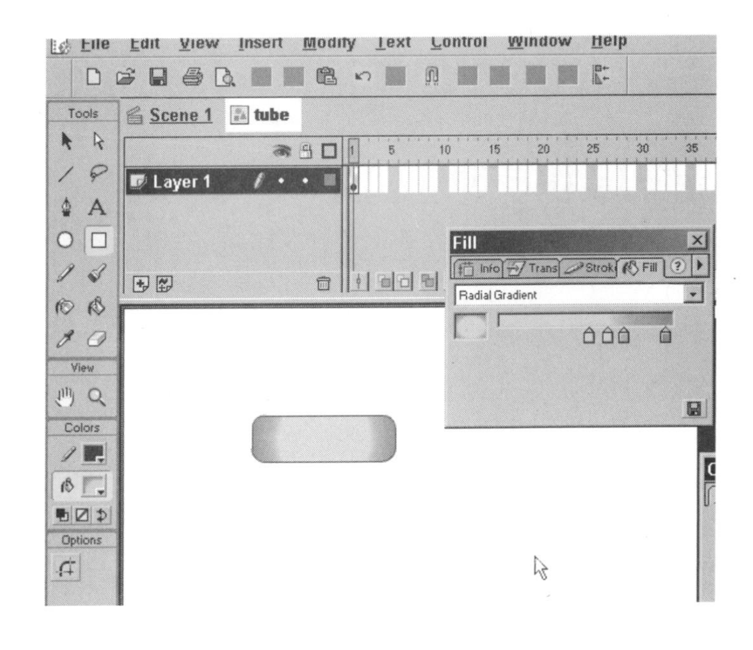

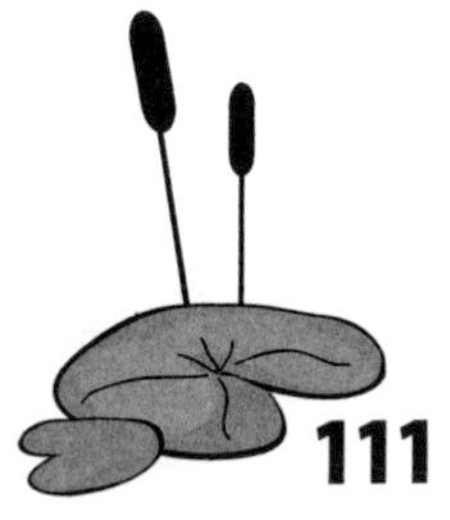

3. Select the button and choose Insert ➢ Convert to Symbol. Name the button "goldone." Select Button in the Behavior section of the Symbol Properties window.

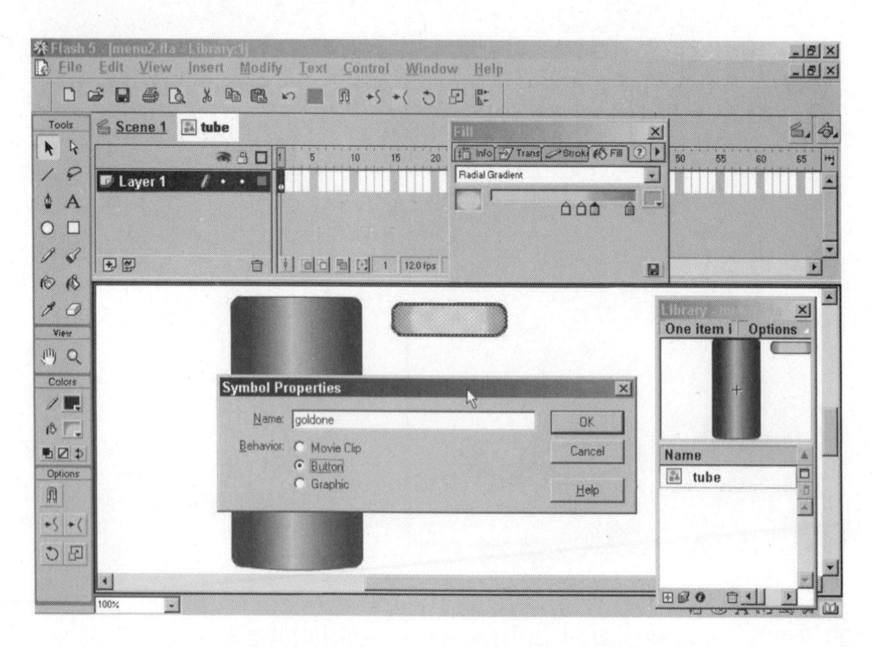

4. Drag the goldone button from the Library window onto the Stage next to the cylinder. Continue dragging copies of the button until you have four buttons stacked vertically to the right of the blue cylinder.

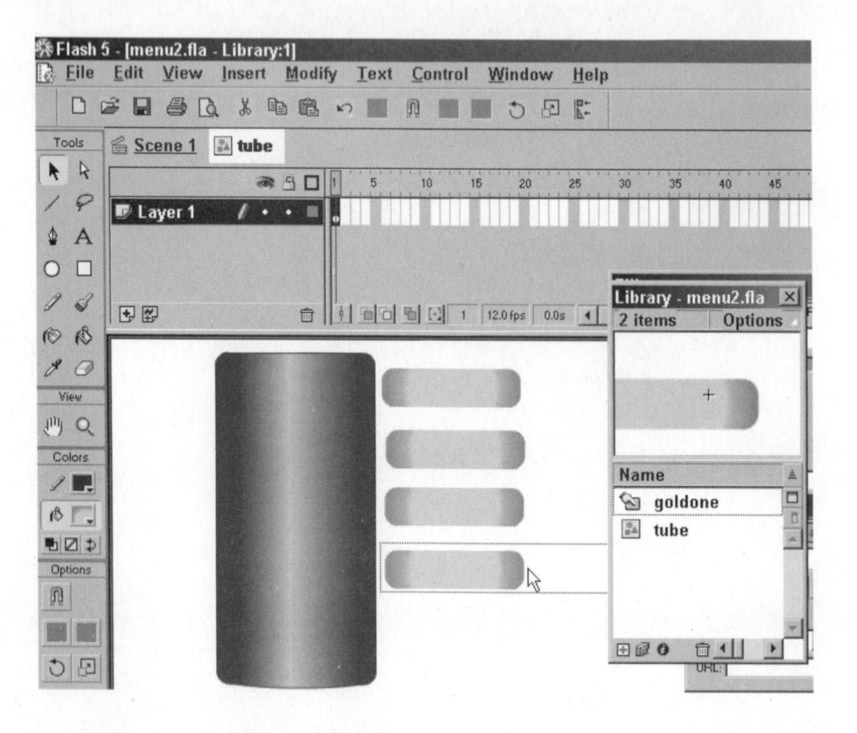

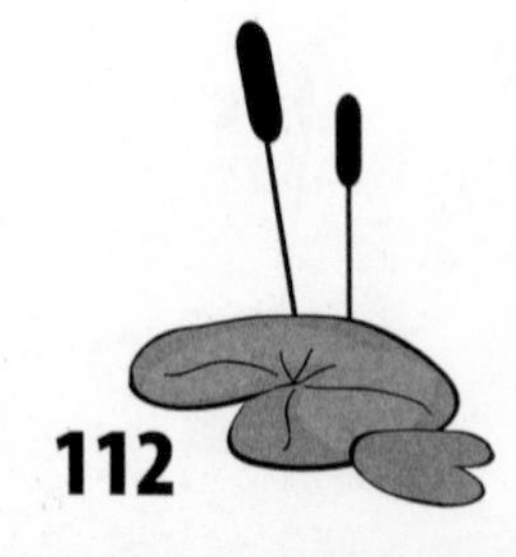